SCORCHED EARTH

SCORCHED EARTH

RESTORING THE COUNTRY AFTER OBAMA

MICHAEL SAVAGE

CENTER
STREET®

NEW YORK   BOSTON   NASHVILLE

Center Street
Hachette Book Group
1290 Avenue of the Americas, New York, NY 10104
centerstreet.com
twitter.com/centerstreet

First Edition: September 2016

Center Street is a division of Hachette Book Group, Inc. The Center Street name and logo are trademarks of Hachette Book Group, Inc.

The publisher is not responsible for websites (or their content) that are not owned by the publisher.

The Hachette Speakers Bureau provides a wide range of authors for speaking events. To find out more, go to www.HachetteSpeakersBureau.com or call (866) 376-6591.

Book design by Timothy Shaner, NightandDayDesign.biz

ISBNs: 978-1-4555-6824-6 (hardcover), 978-1-4555-4162-1 (large type), 978-1-4555-6823-9 (ebook)

Printed in the United States of America

RRD-C

10 9 8 7 6 5 4 3 2 1

Roman civilization did not pass peacefully away. It was assassinated.

—André Piganiol, French scholar

CONTENTS

CONTENTS

CONTENTS

PREFACE

WHY THIS BOOK— AND WHY NOW?

In my book *Government Zero*, I warned that our nation is in danger from two forces: liberals and their progressive agenda, and radical Islamists with their murderous visions of jihad. Each group is working toward similar ends: to destroy Western civilization and remake it in their own respective images of socialism and sharia law.

When I published that book last fall, those two dark forces were well on their way to transforming our once free republic into a third-world dictatorship ruled by Government Zero: absolute government and zero representation.

Today, the situation is even more dire. We are not just being ripped apart by terrorists and socialist politicians, we are seeing pockets of our once great population descending into anarchy.

Inspired by a president and an attorney general who openly censured our brave police, a band of black supremacist, white-hating lunatics ambushed and executed heroic officers in Dallas this past July. It happened again days later in Baton Rouge. Shortly before that, claiming allegiance to ISIS, a Muslim terrorist shot up a gay nightclub in Orlando, murdering scores of people. The end of Western civilization is no longer a vision for enemies within and without. It is operational. They are *doing* it.

The misguided, deceitful, often hateful policies that brought us here are explained in this book. The players in this horror—Barack Hussein Obama, Eric Holder, Loretta Lynch, and now Hillary Clinton—are exposed as the fear-mongering opportunists they are, filled with contempt for success and tradition, pandering to the manufactured cry of "diversity" in order to divide and erode this once great nation. Their goal? To consolidate power forever in their corrupt oligarchy.

But there are also solutions within these pages, though we had better act swiftly if we are to survive.

You see, there *is* a glimmer of hope. Not a bright one, but a start. We—the people, the patriots—are beginning to fight back. The unprecedented rise of Donald Trump has been the spearhead of this rebellion. Whatever the outcome of this election, we have told the entrenched liberal establishment that we don't like the direction the country is headed in. We can, and will, fight as hard as the enemy to preserve our union.

But those of you who are regular listeners to my radio program, *The Savage Nation*, know that this cause, the fight on the barricades, did not begin with Donald Trump.

It began with Michael Savage.

I'm not being immodest. It's a fact. For twenty-two years my message has been borders, language, and culture. My last three to four nonfiction books, if you look at them, were my solutions for saving America. Many of their bullet points or talking points have been and are being used by the Trump campaign, to the credit of Donald Trump and, of course, to the benefit of the United States of America.

I'm going to take credit—not for getting out the vote, I certainly wouldn't take credit for that—but for being the architect of Trump's messaging. Donald Trump first appeared on my radio program in 2011. During his many, many appearances on the show over the years, and also on his campaign positions page, he has reiterated several of my longtime signature themes, including U.S.-China trade reform, Veterans Administration reforms, tax reform, Second Amendment rights, and immigration reform, as priorities. On the day he announced he was entering the ring for the GOP presidential nomination, he hit hard the idea that illegal aliens coming into the United States across the southern border sometimes bring crime with them. That statement, maligned by the corrupt, leftist mainstream media, gave his campaign traction. It was the launching pad that propelled him over his pandering, politically cowardly rivals.

Yet three years earlier, I had said the same thing to a listener on that very issue.

"Wouldn't a sane and rational society select the types of immigrants it wants, rather than a willy-nilly wholesale amnesty for thirty million, many of whom don't even work?" I asked.

I went on to talk about the 30 percent of prisoners in the United States who are illegal aliens. This message was picked up and repeated by the Trump campaign. And we saw it in action in the Brexit vote, when the United Kingdom voted to save itself from the one-way ticket to oblivion which is the Soviet-style European Union. Seventeen million voters said "enough" to setting out the welcome mat for people who call themselves refugees but many of whom are in reality Islamic terrorist infiltrators or sharia-law supporters and took the United Kingdom out of that suicidal scheme.

Don't be fooled, by the way, by the claims that Great Britain has isolated itself economically from the rest of Europe. That's nonsense, and everyone knows it. The United Kingdom is going to go the way of Switzerland. Switzerland isn't part of the European Union because the Swiss are smart. They always remain neutral, and their borders, language, and culture have remained intact. And here's the most important thing: they've negotiated treaties with the European Union. They trade with it. They just don't take orders from a bunch of autocrats sitting in Brussels. They don't want to be told how a small chocolate shop in Zurich should be run!

Some pundits are saying that there is no parallel between the Brexit vote and the Trump revolution here. They say that the demographics are different. Really? Anger is anger anywhere in the world, but I can play the demographics game too: when Donald Trump runs against Hillary Clinton in November, anarchy, crime, chronic joblessness, ongoing terrorism, dysfunctional government, and everything else that fueled Brexit will fuel the electorate. Unless the Republicans shoot themselves in the foot as they did with Mittens Romney, this one is theirs to lose.

I mentioned borders, language, culture. That's been my message for twenty-two years. Tell me how that differs from Donald Trump's defining slogan, "Make America Great Again"? It's almost the same message. Fundamentally, "Make America Great Again" means we must secure our borders, conduct our business and vote in the same language—English—and embrace a common culture. We all know that. Except for the 30-plus million illegal—excuse me, "undocumented"—aliens who are in our country collecting welfare and food stamps, turning communication into a Tower of Babel, and spurning our traditions while promoting their own. Remember the Mexican children who were waving the flag in our homeland while cursing Donald Trump in Spanish during the primaries? Welcome to the new America. Welcome to the new revolution.

My warnings are finally being heeded—hopefully in time.

INTRODUCTION

IT CAN HAPPEN HERE

I was recently in an antiques store in Beverly Hills. I was looking at this and that, Chinese stuff, French stuff. As many of you know, my tastes are very eclectic. Everyone else on the street was closed during the holiday—it was open. The owner and I talked over a Chinese incense burner, the price of it, for a while. By the way the owner looked and the way he spoke, I knew he was from the Middle East. As we talked, one word led to another and the guy finally told me he had been in an Iranian prison for two years. I don't remember exactly how it came up.

I said, "What, during Khomeini's reign of terror? The one that Jimmy Carter brought on by failing to stand up to that zealot?"

The man didn't believe that I knew all of that. He didn't know who I was.

He seemed reluctant to answer at first. It's a habit people acquire when they live in brutally repressive regimes. So I repeated, "Ayatollah Khomeini did that to you?"

He finally said, "Yes."

His answer made me sick. Not just because there are ideological tyrants running nations like Iran but because cowardly liberalism had put him in jail for two years.

"I was twenty years old," he went on. "Do you know what my crime was?"

I asked, "What? What did you do?"

He said, "At the time, Israelis were being killed by Palestinian murderers, suicide bombers, so the Israelis were trying to raise money for bomb-sniffing dogs. I sent four hundred dollars to Israel to help them train a bomb-sniffing dog. Then," he continued, "my second crime against the state of Iran when the Muslim murderers took over was this: they shot the most successful Iranian Jewish businessman in Iran, killed him for no reason, and I went to retrieve his body. They charged me for the bullets, and then they tried me for crimes against the state. The two stated charges were: I paid for a bomb-sniffing dog in Israel, and I retrieved the body of a traitor. They put me in a dark cell for two years. I came to America in 1979 with three hundred dollars in my pocket. I've been working every day of my life to survive since then—and I don't complain about it."

I looked into this man's eyes, unashamedly and openly admiring his unbroken spirit, and I asked, "Sir, how many years had your family been in Iran?"

It caught him by surprise because it's an odd question for an Iranian, as any Persian or Iranian would understand. It's the kind of question you ask in America, where most families have been here only a few generations.

"I don't know," he said. "About twenty-five hundred years?"

If you think of the magnitude of the question and his answer, you can begin to understand what could happen to you in this country because of the community organizer Barack Hussein Obama and women like Hillary Rodham Clinton. If a family can be shattered and displaced after two and a half millennia for a politically unsanctioned act, think of what can happen in a younger country with an equally rabid ideology of sociopolitical correctness.

If you think it can't happen here, my friends, think again. Those who do not know their history are condemned to repeat it.

SCORCHED EARTH

1

OUR SCORCHED EARTH

LIFE UNDER TRUMP, DEATH UNDER CLINTON

Barack Obama has spent nearly eight years working to undermine the United States. And what is astonishing to me is that in spite of his criminal behavior, Hillary Clinton had the nerve to say to Donald Trump, "Start behaving like a president." She was the secretary of state for this dictator! And now she wants four more years of Obama policies.

But let's begin at the beginning. Mao Tse-tung is the model for several of Barack Obama's chief staff members. They've even said so. Oh, people have called them Marxists. They've called them Leninists. This is true, as far as it goes: they're communists. But those commentators don't quite understand that the Obamaists are more politically associated with Mao Tse-tung than anyone else.

Many of you have come out of colleges where you were subjected to brainwashing. This goes back to your elementary school days: brainwashing on what to think about gays;

brainwashing on what to think about global warming; brainwashing on what to think about illegal aliens. But it's all brainwashing. The president himself has said that his daughters know that global warming is real and that the future generation will embrace this more than the current generation. That concept comes right out of Mao.

What does that have to do with Barack Obama? After all, if we buy the popular mythology perpetrated by the press, he's a nice Christian man. But is he really a nice Christian man? Is that why he's flooding America with illegal aliens? Is that why he's flooding America with Muslims? Is that why he doesn't follow the law? Is that why he gets away with virtually anything? Because he's a nice Christian man?

There's only one man who's telling the truth about this issue, and that's Donald Trump. How much longer Trump will get away with it, given the hatred coming at him from the low-life coelenterates in the media, is a question of how strong he really is.

I hope he can take it. I have had to build up a resistance to the hate from the vermin on the left, the hatred from the George Soros–generated machines of hatred such as Media Matters for America. They are front groups for Maoist organizations that want to destroy the opposition. I have learned how to put up with those insects. But when you take a man like Donald Trump—who is used to being revered and is a member of society and respected at the highest levels, and then suddenly has the media turn on him because they're all a bunch of jackals and cowards—how long can even he stand being ostracized? If not for the Constitution, which Obama has shredded time and again, Trump would not be a beacon; he would be a prisoner in a death camp.

There was a man at a Trump campaign rally saying "Obama's a Muslim," and Trump said, very reasonably, "We're gonna be looking at a lot of different things. A lot of people are saying that. A lot of people are saying bad things are happening out there." Right away, the vermin in the media started saying that Trump is a bad man. And there Hillary was, the head of the Clinton machine—doyenne of the most hide-in-plain-sight criminal activity I've ever seen in my life, which occurred under her watch—daring to say that it's Trump who should start behaving like a president. Well, there is a lot to be said about that, but it's not about Trump. It's about her refusal to confess her own crimes, it's about her refusal to tell us where she was the night Benghazi burned and the ambassador was killed, and many other avoidances. What about the hundreds of millions of dollars funneled into her husband's library from foreign governments and people in America who want favors? Like the Saudis, who don't want their role in the 9/11 terror attacks made public.

Obama is, by definition, a Muslim, unless he converted to Christianity and I don't know about it. His father, Barack Obama, Sr., was a Muslim from Kenya. His stepfather, Lolo Soetoro, was a nominal Muslim. So what is Barry? Well, according to Islamic law, he is a Muslim. It is handed down through patrilineal descent. Now if one in five Americans or more still think he's a Muslim, is it not a valid discussion point? When did he convert to Christianity? When was he last seen going into a church—one other than the forum abused by that hate-baiting anarchist Reverend Jeremiah Wright? Don't you think it's an issue that is worth discussing in a predominantly Christian nation? A more important question might be, why don't the media think it's important? What, do we have to hide the religion of the nation? The founding religion of America has to be hidden? Why is it not hidden in Iran? It's because atheist Maoists run the country. They'd like you to think there is no religion until, one day, the Muslims are the majority and Obama can sit back in his rocking chair, reading the Quran, and finally announce what we've all known for decades.

There's no crime in being Muslim. But how do you argue with facts? If your father is a Muslim and you go to a Muslim school as a child, you are a Muslim unless you convert to another religion. So he obviously had to have converted to Christianity somewhere along the way because he was a devout churchgoer. For twenty years he went to Reverend Wright's church, where he learned to hate America and learned to hate everything about America. So he is a Christian of that order, which would be a liberation theologist—a communist—along the order of Pope Francis, which is why that pope was invited to America. But not Benjamin Netanyahu, who is the leader of another state being assaulted by hateful Muslims.

Now, unlike the Obama administration, let's be fair and clear on this point: Not all Muslims are against the principles of democracy. Many of them are trying to destroy ISIS. The Muslim president of Egypt, the sixth largest Muslim country in the world, is trying to destroy ISIS. But Obama will not help him. The king of Jordan is a Muslim. But Obama will not send him the heavy weapons he needs to combat ISIS. He will not arm the Kurds in Iraq, who are heroically fighting ISIS.

Why is that? Can someone really hate America and Christianity so much that he is willing to stand by and let them be decapitated and crucified rather than send arms to regional allies?

It's not a question of whether Obama is a Muslim. It's a question of what kind of Muslim he is. Many have said he's a front man for the Muslim Brotherhood, the outlaw terrorist group that briefly held power in Egypt. I've gotten emails from people in the highest levels of the intelligence world who are no longer in the government, having all been purged as was done under Josef Stalin, who swear that the Muslim Brotherhood is running this country.

When this kind of fear starts to bubble up from the people, I've got to tell you there's a prairie fire, to use a leftist phrase. Yes, my Democrat leftist friends, there is a prairie fire burning, not on the question of whether Obama is a Muslim but about which side he is on.

So on to the next question: what kind of Islam does he practice? Well, let's see. He's the only president who doesn't even pretend to go to church on Sunday. I mean, you have to give credit to Hillary and Bill. Despite shattering most of the Ten Commandments, Bill would chuckle his way into a church on Sunday. At least he pretended to be a practicing Christian to satisfy all the little people out there who in his mind actually go to church and believe in it.

Obama doesn't even make the pretense. He doesn't pretend to be a Christian. How would you know he's a Christian? By what act? Tell me how you would know what his religion is. Does it matter? I think it does matter, especially when we're under assault by radical Islam and he won't even say it's radical Islam. I think it's an important question, at a time when radical Islam is on the march, to know where our president stands.

I asked my housekeeper, who's from El Salvador and speaks Spanish and some English, "Do you think that Obama is a Muslim?" She's a devout Christian, a churchgoer, believes in Jesus. She said, "He is a serpent." She used the Spanish word for "serpent." I was actually stunned. So maybe he isn't a Muslim or even a Maoist. Maybe he's a serpent, like the one that slithered through the Garden of Eden.

So where does Maoist, Muslim Barack Hussein Obama leave us when he finally leaves office to make another apology tour through the Muslim nations, this time as a paid speaker instead of as president? Maybe he'll stop in London and apologize to its new Muslim mayor for the American Revolution. He likes bowing to Muslim leaders.

Obama will leave us at a dangerous crossroads as a nation. And many of us know it. We know that the lowly night crawlers who run the new world order spearheaded by Soros and the anarchists of Black Lives Matter and other nihilists have chosen America for a certain destiny and that we, the people, are the last chance we have to save ourselves. Who is there to choose the right path for America? It's certainly not the corrupt Hillary Clinton, who never met a lie she couldn't embrace. It could be Donald Trump. If he can survive the onslaughts of the left wing, he just might save the nation.

You might remember the dialog I alluded to earlier between one of Trump's supporters and Trump. The supporter asked a question: "We have a problem in this country. It's called Muslims. We know our current president is one."

"Right," Trump said.

"You know he's not even an American," the supporter went on.

"We need this first—we need this first question . . ." Trump said.

"But anyway, we have training camps growing where they want to kill us."

"Mm-hm," Trump said.

"That's my question. When can we get rid of them?"

"We're going to be looking at a lot of different things," Trump told him. "And you know, a lot of people are saying that, and a lot of people are saying that bad things are happening out there. We're going to be looking at that and plenty of other things."

What's wrong with that? Maybe the better question to ask is, is anything wrong with that exchange? How many years have we talked about the Muslim training camps around America, the camps where they're training with guns on country properties? It's a fact. There are several in New York State. We've reported on them. New York state troopers know about them.

So Trump is on to Muslim Obama, and so is a large segment of the rightly concerned American population. What about in Washington? Many people in the intelligence community say Obama's helping the Muslim Brotherhood, that they're running the country, instructing the FBI, and instructing the CIA. We could probably confirm it if it became a big enough issue. Trump is the only one who didn't say, "Oh, no no no no. Oh, get that guy out of here. No no no. We can't even touch that question." It shows you that Trump's not afraid of any question. He's a freethinker. He's a free man. And so those who belong to the kingdom of Obama, those who have created the new empire, will immediately say that's an illegitimate question. He said, "Well, we'll look into that." And there are plenty of other things out there to look into.

That's why Obama and his minions are fiercely opposing Trump, because he's not using the same playbook, which is in danger of becoming the prayer book of America. The playbook of a one-man, Maoist Muslim governance. He is the only one who's saying, "No, I'm not playing by your rules. I'm playing by America's rules. I'm not playing by the rule of Mao Tse-tung under Obama. I am going to make sure that America is great again, not that I am great again."

Barack Obama. Maybe we should just call him Maobama. Or Obamao.

Like Obama, Mao never admitted he was wrong. He killed his lieutenant who had been with him from the early days, the man who had gone on the Long March with him. He saved the most horrendous torture for his closest ally, who told him, "What you've done is wrong. You've killed twelve million Chinese through your agricultural policies. Your plans are not working. Whatever you've touched has turned to garbage."

Sort of like Obamacare and the fake war on ISIS, right? You see the pattern here?

This is why frightened but right-thinking people turn to someone like Donald Trump, who will protect their ideals. If you were to define Donald Trump's politics, you would not say that he's a nativist; you would say that he's a nationalist. Nationalism respects national traditions and calls for duty and sacrifice. At its best, it's like religion in its ability to inspire a strong, charitable sense of community in its followers— far more effectively than the community disorganizer who became president. All that, I have to tell you, is anathema to the new world order. It's why Trump scares its members.

Getting back to something I mentioned earlier: if you put the pieces together, you can see why Obamao hates Israel. The answer, as I've been saying, is that Trump and Israel stand for nationalism. The only nationalisms permitted in Obamao's world view are Muslim nationalism and black liberation nationalism. Islamo-nationalism is acceptable because there are too many Muslims for Israel to take on right now. But, you see, Israel's small. There are not that many Jews.

So there's one presidential candidate who's a nationalist, and his opponents are holding back nothing in trying to destroy him and his candidacy.

Let me tell you a tale of two countries. The two countries are the free and prosperous United States if Donald Trump is elected president and the soulless welfare state the United States will become if Hillary Clinton wins. On one level, I can't even believe we're discussing the prospect of Hillary winning.

Remember when Clinton said to Trump, "Start behaving like a president." Well, Michael Savage says to Clinton, "Stop behaving so high and mighty when you are a liar and perjurer."

If Hillary wins, she'll be one thing more. Like her boss before her, she'll be a dictatorial traitor. The Fourth Estate was afraid to attack a black president. Do you think it will be any better with a woman in the Oval Office? She won't have to censor the media to take control and create a state-run press: they'll do it for her. Look at the *New York Times*, which self-righteously proclaimed at the end of June that the GOP Benghazi commission had found no evidence of "wrongdoing" by Hillary. Now, there's a slippery word. Did it mean legal wrongdoing or moral wrongdoing? It couldn't have meant the latter, because that report was full of reprehensible neglect for the safety of our diplomats and undercover military on the ground there. How can you think otherwise when you learn that not a single military asset was moved to the region when our compound was under assault?

So what happens on day one of a Trump administration? The economy-crushing burden of Obamacare: gone. The small-business-crushing taxes of Obama: gone. The threat of ISIS: on the way out. Our porous borders: sealed. As a result of those acts, the jobless rate starts to shrink. The debt shrinks, too.

What happens on day one of a Hillary Clinton administration? None of the above. Did you hear me? Those things that even a kid in elementary school knows are so urgently needed *do not happen*.

She will continue the Obama doctrine, which has determined that America will no longer exist as a sovereign nation. It's being gutted from within, not so much by political figures but by thieves using political operatives called senators to do trade deals that are against the best interests of the nation. That's how China grew so quickly. It grew on our back. Remember when Clinton was exporting factories to China? The Chinese were buying whole factories out of the Midwest. They took every machine tool to China. You don't remember how Clinton sacked America, do you?

What else happens on day one of a Hillary Clinton administration? How about an energy supply disaster? Under Hillary, coal and natural gas will vanish as energy sources. Hydrofracking and coal burning will be made illegal. What will we get instead? Solar and wind energy. The solar and the wind companies, which contribute heavily to the Democrats, are going to get their payback. And look what happens if you don't invest in solar and wind energy: you go to jail. Businesses and private individuals who don't pay the carbon tax will go to jail. And all the electronic locks in the prisons will be solar powered.

Most private individuals, home owners, can't afford and don't get enough benefits from solar and wind energy to make it worth their while. If this goes through, though, there are going to be fewer private individuals. All the jobs from natural gas and coal are going to go away, along with the small businesses that will have to struggle to meet payroll after the Bernie Sanders minimum wage boost goes into effect.

Maybe that's part of the plan—the plan for a socialist state like the one Bernie Sanders wanted. What do you think will happen to the price of your coffee, your cheeseburger, when your waitress has to make $15 an hour? They'll be more expensive, and you'll wait for them longer, because when small businesses have to pay that minimum wage they're going to cut staff, cut jobs.

Those workers are going to become wards of the Clinton welfare state. But at least they'll be able to smoke marijuana, which will be legal for recreational use. And it'll keep the people stupid, because that's what marijuana does. You better believe that if Clinton gets elected, she's not gonna inhale, either. She wants all of you to be stupid, but she's too smart for that—she's not gonna inhale.

You can hope that the natural course of things, the will of the people, will be enough to correct all this in four years if Hillary wins. When the Democrats met to assemble their platform, one of the planks the Bernie faction called for was to cap donations to candidates and use public financing. Right. Because they're scared that the people will know what's right and support conservative candidates. They can't have that, so they try to cut off the money supply. Thankfully, not even the Democrats are willing to give up political donations. See, the Democrats know when Bernie from Brooklyn goes too far, and it's when his ideas start messing with their money.

This new world order will be Maoism merged with post-9/11 Islamic jihad. It's stronger than you could ever imagine. The leftist power brokers—Ted Kennedy, Howard Dean, John Kerry, and John Edwards—inserted Obama into the

White House, and now all of a sudden, just as the Left is about to complete their act, along comes a billionaire who is a nationalist and they don't know what to do other than to smear him. They're doing to him everything they've done to everyone in the media who has stood up to President Zero. They figured that we're marginal figures, we're not important, we have no power. But now a man comes along who just might save the country, might save the nation's sovereignty.

So Obama leaves Hillary a legacy and a playbook. Let's step back and see what the contents look like. Bear with me, because it's the kind of chess game only a psychotic Harvard progressive professor could have conceived.

Iran, a Shia nation, Obama is on its side. ISIS, a Sunni terrorist organization, he's on its side. Israel, a free Jewish democracy, he hates it. And we'll get more of that hate under Hillary. One of Bernie Sanders's supporters, Cornel West, tried to insert language into the Democrat platform calling for "an end to occupation and illegal settlements in Palestinian territory." Right. That failed, thankfully, but don't be fooled: Democrats are anti-Israel.

So what is Obama really doing in the Mideast? Well, you could say it's quite rational. He's pitting Sunni against Shia, and he wants them to kill each other. That would be one theory, but I don't think that's the actuality of it. Let's look at Syria. What's he doing in Syria? Iran, a Shia nation, is a supporter of Bashar al-Assad, the despotic ruler of Syria. Iran and Russia are on the same side. They want to take out ISIS because ISIS opposes the Shia theocracy. They want a Sunni theocracy. Which side are we on? We don't know. Obama refuses to really join Russia in the war against ISIS. He's in a quandary there. First he supported Iran with the nuclear deal. Now that Iran and Russia are unifying as allies against ISIS and Syria to support Assad, suddenly Obama has cold feet. He put on the brakes.

So he took a seat at this chess board and made his moves, but I have to ask: Does he really know what he's doing? Can you conceptualize that it's a bunch of college idiots who don't even know what the hell they're doing—that these hysterical sorority girls take it a day at a time? And then when they get caught they cover it up with the government media complex, which makes them look so intelligent. Do they really know what they're doing? I don't know. Maybe they do. Maybe they're much smarter than you think. Maybe they're much stupider than you think. But we have a right as Americans to ask, where do their loyalties lie? After all, we're fighting for our survival right now. Whether you know it or not, you are facing an existential crisis for the rest of your life. Will this nation be taken over by the Muslim Brotherhood in a stealth manner, as many say it already has at the upper levels of government? Will your children be forced to bow to Allah in their lifetime?

You don't think that's a rational question? About 20 percent of the American people do. What would you like to do? Put them in prison camps? Would you like to erase their minds? Would you like to make it Year Zero for them? Would you like to take the 20 percent or 25 percent of Americans who think that Obamao is out to destroy a free America, would you like to execute them? Is that the kind of liberalism you're practicing? No, of course not. Would you like to reeducate them? Of course. That's what you're doing. That's what Obamao and his marching minions are doing.

We've already seen what this future is going to look like in San Francisco and Berkeley. Once liberal cities became bastions of hate, bastions of authoritarianism, bastions of loudmouth radical feminists who took over the cities and shouted down anyone who disagreed with them. And now we have the sad situation of dictatorships in Berkeley, dictatorships in San Francisco, and every other so-called liberal bastion in the United States of America being run like mini–Maoist states. They had the complete reeducation. Newspapers don't exist anymore. The universities and schools are espousing the party line. Whatever the leader says, whatever Chairman Obamao says, they do. Whatever Obamao says, they agree to. They don't question it. They're loyal little soldiers, a loyalty like you've never seen in the history of this fair nation.

We even have reeducation camps. They're called schools and universities. Instead of the drip drip drip of water torture, we have the drone drone drone of mobile devices with voices: they're called the media. Those are the reeducation camps. They don't actually send you to a place to relearn. They don't have to send you anywhere. They took over the places that do the reeducation. So the only things missing now are the actual beatings, arrests, and murders in America. We are living through a very dangerous transition in America right now, and there's only one individual who actually knows what's going on and is willing to say it. He's as clear-eyed on it as I am. Donald Trump. Which is why the Lilliputians of the administration and the media are attacking him.

A very smart man wrote, "Obama does not live like a Muslim. He drinks, he did drugs, he favors gay marriage, but he favors international political Islam."

Of course, a dictator can do what he wants, and Hussein Obama is that. So again the question is, which political side of the Islamic equation is he on? Is he a Shia? The Iranians are Shias. It doesn't fit, does it? Because ISIS is made up largely of the former Republican Guard of Obama's namesake, Saddam Hussein, and they're all Sunnis. The Sunnis who were excommunicated after Saddam was killed by the US military are now raging across the Middle East to regain not only control of Iraq but of the whole Middle East if they can. And they are Sunnis, which is exactly why Iran opposes them.

It's very hard to understand the Sunni-Shia thing. To most Americans, the closest analogy is Catholic-Protestant. That's what it's like, the Catholic-Protestant wars in Ireland, only Sunni-Shia goes back about a thousand years. Islam is the religion of pieces, and what Muslims do is blow themselves up for a thousand years over a tribal dispute. They've done so for a thousand years, and we're bringing them into this country. They're really going to integrate into the Stars and Stripes Forever. Yeah. The scimitar is never going to integrate with the Stars and Stripes.

For those people, it's not about integrating; it's about conforming to their will or being butchered. Mao Tse-tung killed 45 million Chinese who would not conform to his view of the Cultural Revolution.

When your children go to a university and they are forced to accept things that they know are false and to sit there for fear of losing a grade or being thrown out of the classroom, you're watching Maoism in action.

Why bother to talk about communist China right now? Because we hear about the Holocaust as one of the great tragic events of the twentieth century, and it was. Six million Jews were killed by Hitler. About seven million non-Jews were also killed. It was as if the Cambodian communist dictator Pol Pot's genocide were multiplied twenty times over. The biggest part of this story is the Cultural Revolution, when people were forced to conform to what is called political correctness. It came directly from that period of human history. More than 13,000 opponents of Mao Tse-tung's new regime were killed in one region alone in just three weeks. And that was by fellow Chinese. So if you have the illusion that your military will not turn on you, you are crazy. Those of you who think your military is above doing that are nuts. You know nothing about history.

The most important lesson to be learned from this is the actions of the Red Guards, Mao's enforcers. Who were they? Well, his Great Leap Forward led to the massive starvation of Chinese people. Millions of Chinese starved to death because of Mao Tse-tung's insanity. Very much like any other government bureaucrat, he wanted to stamp out his failures. So he created enforcers called Red Guards, an army of children and young idiot adults who were used to kill or beat up anyone not toeing the Maoist line. Teachers were targeted first, as they are today on today's campuses. Any artifacts of Chinese history were targeted. A favorite method of those people was to whip their elders with the heavy metal buckles on their leather belts.

The violence began at the bottom. Everything was very carefully planned at the top. There were constant messages going from the Communist Party to the students. The beatings, the beatings, the beatings. The students first confronted the teachers for not conforming to the political correctness and repeating the big lie, and then the teachers were tortured and killed.

That's a lot of history to digest, but pay careful attention to this part: we are seeing the similar pattern emerging again, like the mobs we have seen in Dallas, Baltimore, Oakland, and Ferguson.

There's only one man on the American political stage who can stop this. I know how things begin, and I know how they end. And unless this madness of political correctness is stopped in this country, the worst is yet to come.

I've documented this because I want to stop the corruption of our borders, language, culture. Vote, while you still can. You think I'm being an alarmist?

Consider this. On September 11, 2001, a mayoral primary was under way in New York City. After the attacks, that election was postponed. Imagine a day when America votes for president. There's an attack, or riots by black nationalists. The election is called off, and, because of the extraordinary nature of the event, President Hillary Clinton assumes unconstitutional authority—like waging retaliatory war without congressional approval. Think that can't happen? Abraham Lincoln did it during the Civil War. The only difference is, Lincoln gave up those powers after the war. That's one reason he was a great president. Does anyone think Hillary would do the same? Do you think fearful, apathetic Americans will raise their voices in protest while Commander in Chief Clinton wages war— and, incidentally, issues executive order after executive order that favors her friends the Saudis, George Soros, and other enemies of freedom?

We are fighting for our life and freedom. Where there's one-man rule, there's a chance for great corruption. Because all you've got to do is buy off a party official above you and he kicks up to the party official above him, and she kicks up to the party official above her, and it goes all the way up to the top. It's very much like organized crime. And that's why we in America enjoyed a great government for a very long period of time until it became what is now: a Ponzi scheme in a criminal empire that runs off one-man rule where there are few checks and balances.

Witness what Chairman O did with the Iran deal. The American people opposed it by a large majority. Only 20 percent supported giving Iran a path to nuclear weapons. Think about that. Where's our representation? Congress opposed it, yet he used quasi-legal maneuvering to support Iran. If that's not one-man rule, I'd like to know what is.

Here is a short list of his crimes and misdemeanors: providing arms to people who would kill Americans, whether they are Arabs in Gaza or the Mexican drug cartels; using the Internal Revenue Service as a political weapon against legitimate nonprofit organizations that dared to oppose him; changing laws by executive action, rather than the way laws are supposed to made or amended: through congressional action—Congress, not the president, is the lawmaking body in this country. We aren't a banana republic—yet. Look at the way he implemented the so-called DREAM immigration law: when Congress didn't go far enough to carry out his agenda, he just executive-ordered it into existence.

We have an openly mad president who is doing everything he can as quickly as he can to decimate everything this country stood for, stands for, and would stand for.

Now let's go down a list of other things that he has done and is doing. That's what really matters. Let's assume that Obama is not a dogmatist, that religion doesn't really matter. Let's remove it from the table for the moment. We have the most powerful military on Earth. Why has he not destroyed ISIS? Do you remember how, after the terrorists took Mosul, they had a victory parade? It ran about a half a mile long with Toyota trucks with machine guns on them, a long line through the desert. Well, if President George W. Bush had seen it, you would have seen a highway of death. You would have seen charred corpses on top of the Toyota trucks. They wouldn't be doing war cries today. But Obama didn't even have one missile fired at that convoy. That said it all to me. That was the end of the story. Hussein Obama wasn't going to lift a finger to defend Christianity or stop Islamic terror.

I have every reason to tell you, again, that we're fighting for survival—personal survival, national survival, we're fighting for it. I want my granddaughter to grow up in a free America. I don't want her bowing down to Mecca. I don't want her bowing down to some cretin in the White House, some snake, some serpent. I don't want her to be afraid to be a freethinker like her grandfather. That's what I'm fighting for.

I get chills up my spine as I write this. Everything is at stake. It's easy to think, ah, you know, these right-wing guys, they're making it worse than it is. It's not that bad. Look, the sky is blue, the clouds are white. I can watch a basketball game tonight. Well, you can do all of those things and also be an ignorant moron. You can be worth hundreds of millions of dollars and be a political moron. You can be an ignoramus. You can be making a million dollars a minute and be a moron. I've met many of them. They don't even know what's going on in front of their eyes.

HILLARY CLINTON: CRIME AND NO PUNISHMENT

What do you call someone who is so corrupt, so demonstrably incompetent, and so completely unqualified to be President? Longtime readers and listeners to *The Savage Nation* know the answer to that.

Hillary Clinton. She would have us believe that she is Grandma Hillary the Benign, the Caring, the Just. But, as Donald Trump has said, she is a liar. A world-class liar. She's like a character from a heist movie where someone is trying to rob a casino or steal a diamond. Only in this case, she's looking to hijack America.

This woman—who gives expensive speeches to Wall Streeters and then refuses to release the transcripts—this political harpy has sold her soul to the Left in order to fend off that old Kremlinite Bernie Sanders and placate Elizabeth Warren, the wicked witch of the Left. Pick one of her speeches, *any* one, and you will hear a litany of victim harvesting.

Whether it's "black lives matter," "the LGBT community," "undocumented aliens," her beloved Syrian refugees or polar bears impacted by the myth of global warming, she is constantly shoving them in our faces as examples of things we should care about.

The economy? Terrorism? Brexit and its impact on the world—including states like Texas threatening to do the same, leave our union? Those, she says, are fearmongering issues of the Republicans. They're not real threats.

Like her naive, destructive commander in chief Barack Hussein Obama, she considers those to be existential threats or the GOP crying wolf.

But let's look at her record, what she's actually done instead of what she says.

On the air, I have spent a great deal of time speculating about Grandma Hillary waging unconstitutional war as president. But the truth is, we don't have to speculate. We know exactly what she's going to do. She's already done it. Clinton's first war was in Libya, while she was still secretary of state. Do you fully understand the chaos that unleashed? While she was celebrating the death of Muammar Gaddafi, hundreds of thousands of African Arab refugees were being released into the world. She made Libya safe, all right: safe for people who could take over its resources and use them against their liberators.

Before 2011 and the "Day of Rage" in that fractured nation, Libya produced 1.8 million barrels of oil a day. That oil was produced by a *secular* republic. Take note of that: it had no religious agenda, no desire to convert or destroy anyone. Then, after the Day of Rage and still under Secretary of State Clinton, the Obamao administration supported the Libyan Muslim Brotherhood rebels with a no-fly zone. Grandma Hillary ignored two proposals to stop the fighting, including one that was passed along to her by the Department of Defense and the Joint Chiefs of Staff. You know: the people who *should* be running our wars. Oil production was off by 80 percent, and what was being produced was benefitting the Libyan Muslim Brotherhood. That is not progress. Those were the seeds of destruction for ourselves and the world. Now Hillary Clinton is asking for four years to water the garden.

Hillary Clinton fought her war using Ahmed Abu Khattala, a Libyan rebel brigade commander, as one of her surrogates. You probably don't know his name. But you know one of his most famous battles: the next time her "pal" was in the news was on September 11, 2012, leading an attack on the US diplomatic compound in Benghazi that left Ambassador J. Christopher Stevens dead. A casualty in Hillary Clinton's war.

You remember all the lying, treasonous nonsense she spewed when she told us that the embassy attack was spontaneous, the result of an amateur film about Muhammad—when she knew it wasn't? She was just warming up the double-talk. Listen to what this destructive scam artist said in June 2016, after Great Britain voted to leave the European Union.

> This time of uncertainty only underscores the need for calm, steady, experienced leadership in the White House to protect Americans' pocketbooks and livelihoods, to support our friends and allies, to stand up to our adversaries, and to defend our interests. It also underscores the need for us to pull together to solve our challenges as a country, not tear each other down.

Experienced leadership? You mean the kind that leaves our people dead in the streets of Benghazi? That allows ISIS to flourish in an unprotected Middle East? That has unleashed millions of refugees from Africa into Europe?

Not to tear each other down! This from the woman who uses every opportunity to denigrate Republicans, the Second Amendment, those of us who decry Obama's abuse of executive orders—which, by the way, the Supreme Court verified by virtue of a four–four tie, letting stand a lower court ruling on his lawless orders on immigration. This woman dares to lecture *us* about tearing each other down?

Hillary is power mad. And if that means pandering to a patchwork of groups that, as little as a decade ago weren't on her radar, then she'll pander. If that means kissing the ring of that street agitator Al Sharpton, she will genuflect and purse her lips.

Once she's in power, a lot of corrupt, anti-American organizations will have been responsible for putting her there. I'll go through a list of some of them later in this book. Read that list carefully, because under President Clinton you'll know some of the people—not all of the people, because we'll never know all of the people she's indebted to. And she's going to owe all of them favors.

2

OUR CHALLENGES

IT IS HAPPENING HERE ALREADY

A timid college professor from Cambodia, Pol Pot, went to Paris to study Marxism. When he returned to his native land, he introduced all the tenets of Marxism to that ancient nation. What happened next was as horrifying as it was astonishing. Within just a few years, mobs of youth called Khmer Rouge had rampaged through the middle class, humiliating, torturing, and killing its most prominent members—doctors, lawyers, teachers, engineers, police chiefs. Anyone with glasses was considered a bourgeois counterrevolutionary. You may remember a movie about this subject called *The Killing Fields*. It depicted the mountains of skulls that were found after the Marxist rampage ended. Two to 3 million Cambodians were worked to death or killed outright by that mob of insane Marxists.

Now, ours isn't a small country. We have about twenty times the population that Cambodia did in the 1970s. But are we immune to the hateful whims of a timid college professor who studied Marxism and then set out to transform his nation? Or does that sound familiar? Does that sound like the insidious process that was started by Barack Obama with his transformation of this great nation into a shadow of its former self?

Pay close attention to what I have written for you in this book, because not only can it happen here, it has been happening here, it *is* happening here. There are not yet mountains of skulls, but there are mountains of dead souls, and that is the beginning of the end of this nation unless it is turned around. No matter who wins this election—even if it's a Republican divorced from the progressive, leftist doctrine of Obama and his cronies—it will be a Herculean task to reverse the damage that this administration has done to all of the fundamental institutions of our great nation through its systematic poisoning of the nation's body politic.

This is a book that is both a warning and a hope—a hope that you elect the right person, because if you elect any Democrat who has been tainted by the Barack Obama, Bernie Sanders, Elizabeth Warren form of socialism, it's inevitable that this downward spiral will continue and there will be no stopping it. The process that began with the affirmative actioning of America, the feminization of America, and the LGBT mainstreaming of America is not only growing, it has a new fellow poster child: the Islamization of America. Even if we don't wind up with actual Islamic sharia law once the Muslim in the White House leaves, we'll wind up with something like it: liberal-fascism codes of behavior that control both public and private activities and limit our actions in our own homes and the freedoms guaranteed to us under the Constitution and the Bill of Rights.

In the following pages, you will see what happened to Iran when it was Islamized, what happened to Iraq when it was Islamized, what happened to Lebanon when it was Islamized, and what happens to any and every nation that permits itself to be taken over by fanatics.

Read carefully.

THE DECAY OF AMERICAN CULTURE

What happened to our beloved America?

I know what's happening *now*. We have let in a sea of cancers—some of them our "progressive" elected officials— that are eating us up from within. The question is, how did we get here?

Nearly a half century ago, we put a man on the moon. Now leftist protesters reveal their full moon in broad daylight on New York City streets. With no help from Al Gore, despite his ridiculous claims, we Americans invented the information superhighway. Internet entrepreneurs created companies such as eBay, thereby accelerating global commerce. Now we have congressmen of both political parties texting underage boys and tweeting out pictures of their appendage to young girls.

How did we decline so rapidly?

The only certain thing is that America's wounds are internal. And that has left us vulnerable to attack externally. Radical Islamists are determined to kill us and wipe Great Satan America and Little Satan Israel off the map. ISIS, Iran, al-Qaeda, Boko Haram, Hamas, Hezbollah, and Saudi

Arabian Wahhabi nutcases all want to destroy us. The World War II generation faced threats head-on. Now, through inactivity or liberal self-loathing, we help those who are trying to kill us.

Take the Iran nuclear deal, which gave more than $100 billion to a nation chanting for our destruction every day. Not just chanting but working on it in heavily fortified nuclear bunkers and in hidden sheds where IEDs are built to kill our soldiers. How insane have we become? Iranians in Tehran yell, "Death to America!" We respond by giving them the tools to carry out their wishes. The Greatest Generation defeated the Nazis and communism. Now radical Muslims are threatening us and uncaring, oblivious, Bernie Sanders–supporting millennials are too busy Instagramming and shminstagramming to fight. Islamists watch training videos on how to carry out jihad against the infidels. Our kids are too busy watching YouTube videos and taking selfies and reducing our language to simplistic bursts of OMG and LOL and WTF. Everything is a selfie, it's about the self. Our enemies are preparing our funerals while our young people worry that pictures of the funerals will not show up on their Instagram accounts.

Through its proxy ISIS, Iran tried, and apparently failed, to set up a global caliphate while we strive to become the next Mozambique, one of the poorest nations on the planet. How did the Islamists go from being a regional power to a global fighting force? How did Americans end up actually *supporting* our enemies?

It starts with a culture that shares a common bond with our enemies. They don't want us to exist, and, sadly, neither do we. Forget good breeding, where we are respectful to one another and don't take major offense at every minor setback. We don't do *any* breeding. Islamists have fourteen children apiece, so losing seven children to homicide bombings is a drop in the bucket. We went from having 2.3 children in every family to an abortion culture and an overpriced Manhattan loft. A three-bedroom family house is a waste when there is no family. Islamists ban birth control and turn their women into baby jihad factories. Their population is expanding exponentially.

London has a Muslim mayor. He got in before the United Kingdom found its full-throated, unified, national voice and left the European Union and its race-shaming assault on the populace. By the way, did you know who his predecessor was? Boris Johnson, the man who lead the Brexit revolt.

Here's something else Muslims in London have: fund-raising advertising on the sides of buses for Islamic Relief. I'd like to know what they're fund raising for. Islamic Relief put the phrase "Glory to Allah" on the sides of buses in London around Ramadan to urge good Muslims to give for whatever its purposes are, and everyone stood aside and watched. I suppose if the buses have Allah's name on them, some Muslims might think twice before blowing them up, right? They'll kill each other, but they won't defame the Prophet or his Maker. Maybe we all just need to walk around with Allah's name on us to be safe. They already had Allah's name on a mosque near the World Trade Center murder site, which was given 24/7 police protection by the taxpayers of New York City. Maybe an Allah storefront or gift ship would stop them from bombing the area a third time. You think I'm kidding? For more than a year, a sign in the window of that insult offered free Qurans in Spanish.

How long before other cities in Europe and the United States have radical Muslim mayors? And senators? Remember these words when you hear about more European nations with Muslim elected officials. We have feminists demanding a life of free sex with unlimited trips to the abortion clinic while our enemies multiply among us in closed towns even our police are afraid to enter. It reminds me of the Mafia communities near where I grew up in New York. The mob policed those streets. No one else was needed—or wanted.

Our declining birthrate is killing us, except for single mothers on welfare who have four, five, six kids by different fathers and get paid per baby. Most people would never connect abortion to radical Islam, but you're smarter than most people.

Don't just take my word for it. Look at the numbers. There are 1.2 billion Muslims in the world. The United States has, at last count, a population of 320 million people: with so many illegals it is tough to get an accurate count. There are roughly four times as many Muslims as Americans. They keep adding to their ranks, and we keep importing illegals because our people eliminate their own babies. At this rate we will go the way of Europistan. Italy has had a declining birthrate in recent years. Europe is finished. Its citizens refuse to reproduce while Islamist women keep churning out the next generation of radical Islamists.

The Centers for Disease Control and Prevention reports that approximately 18 percent of pregnancies in the United States ends in abortion. By rough calculation, that is nearly

100,000 more people than in the entire state of Vermont. Did you hear what I said? We're talking about some three-quarters of a million abortions. Imagine if we woke up one day and found out that all of Vermont was aborted. As tempting as it is not to bring the next Bernie Sanders into the world, think of an entire state just empty. That was in one year. Since *Roe v. Wade* in 1973, 54 million abortions have taken place. We have voluntarily killed off between 15 and 20 percent of today's population. Except for the fatherless kids in poor communities. Like tobacco growers, we pay to keep those impoverished, failed families coming. They add to the progressive ranks, to the future of the socialist movement.

The next time you hear a leftist say that illegals do the jobs Americans refuse to do, just remember how many Americans we killed off. Had those babies been born, there would be no labor shortage today. Their children and grandchildren could have joined the US military. Instead, Islamists are breeding and Americans are bleeding. It's easy for Islamists to chant "Death to America!" We have eliminated one-fifth of their obstacles, made their job 20 percent easier.

At least some Americans are still having children. Unfortunately, many of those children spend their formative years being taught how to surrender. The emasculation of American boys is one step short of suicide. Muslims are living in patriarchal societies while American boys are emasculated, raised not even by mothers in many cases but by nannies who are busy texting while they push baby carriages.

Schoolyards used to be filled with kids at recess playing games like "kill the guy with the ball." Nobody died. Boys played with G.I. Joes and girls played with Barbie dolls. Kids played freeze tag without a single incident of sexual harassment. Not long ago, I heard about a young boy who was suspended from school for blowing a girl a kiss on the bus.

Not too many years ago, cartoons were filled with violence. Bugs Bunny tied a gun barrel in a knot and Elmer Fudd's gun went kaboom, covering his own head in black soot. Wile E. Coyote chased the Road Runner and fell off a cliff to his destruction. We as children watched Superman cartoons, but we knew not to try and jump off the roof.

Teenage boys watched Rocky and Rambo and Conan films. Then they went home without trying to kill anybody. Some of us started lifting weights and working out so we could become buff like Stallone or Schwarzenegger. We did not need liberals to tell us the difference between pretend and real life. Common sense and our parents handled that.

Now schools across the country are canceling gym class. Dodgeball apparently promotes aggression, and insurance companies worry that climbing a rope or vaulting a horse will leave schools open to lawsuits. Even rock-paper-scissors is too violent. Rocks and scissors could be used by children to harm each other. Paper requires murdering trees.

It's no wonder that Islamists produce strapping young men while America produces sensitive crybabies and metrosexuals who use "product" in their hair and lather up with expensive body wash. Muslim children are taught hate in madrassas. They are taught how to kill infidels and the blasphemers. American boys are suspended from school for arranging their school lunch vegetables in the shape of a gun. Perhaps it's good they get suspended. Michelle Obama is starving our children anyway. Pizza, burgers, and fries are replaced with gluten-free, calorie-free, flavor-free garbage that the kids throw away. Then they race home or run to a fast-food joint and grab a hamburger because growing boys want more than an apple slice and a fiber protein bar.

During World War II, young boys volunteered to go overseas to save the world. The Korean War had Colonel David Hackworth teaching our young military how best to "kill a Commie for mommy." Now American kids on college campuses retreat to their safe spaces to escape from potential microagressions. Islamists cut off heads and limbs and our young boys shriek at the drop of a microaggression. And we haven't seen the worst of it. Virtual-reality glasses and helmets are coming, with programs and games that will immerse us in a fantasy environment of our choosing. What will happen to our youth then? They'll be fighting in some first-person shooter game while real shooters walk right up to them and put a bullet in the front of their skull.

When I watch movies and TV shows from the 1950s, I see an America that was bold, daring, macho, unafraid, and proud of itself. When I look at America today, I see something else. This is because a very small band of radical fanatical leftists have seized every aspect of the media and every avenue of government imaginable. They're ashamed of the very idea of American exceptionalism. They are not the majority, and they don't speak for the people. They are a group of political deviants. They are political deviants in a statistical sense, a political sense, and a social sense. This small band of deviants in government and in the media has wrecked the United States of America and turned us into a nation of near slaves.

These craven apologists have turned the grandchildren of the Greatest Generation into jellyfish less brave than the average Frenchman. It is easy to blame the 1960s, flower power, and the radicals that spawned them—nihilistic forces such as the Black Panthers and the Weather Underground. It takes a village of people to destroy a child, and they need to be called out by name. Yet Hillary Clinton and Barack Obama are just symptoms of a much bigger disease.

What we're living through right now is part of the disease the cultural revolution started around the time Barry Soetoro was born. This cultural revolution was begun by Allen Ginsberg, Timothy Leary, and Bella Abzug. That was a group that you could never find in hell itself to do more damage to a nation. At least Benedict Arnold was a war hero before he turned traitor. Those people were born agitators. They were all born silk-smooth salespeople of destruction. One pushed rampant sex with animals. Another one pushed rampant drug use, mainly LSD. The other one, God knows what she pushed: a demented mash-up of feminism and socialism. There was also a lawyer involved, William Kunstler. He leapt to the defense of anyone who burned, spit on, or defaced something clean and good.

Abzug once said, "The establishment is made up of little men, very frightened." Of course they were frightened. Long before fire-breathing dragon ladies such as Hillary Clinton and Debbie Wasserman Schultz set about castrating the entire male population, Helen Thomas and Bella Abzug existed. As the self-titled dean of the White House Press Corps, Thomas was more of an Islamist than a feminist. Her demands that Jews be expelled from the Middle East and returned to Europe made her more of a jihadist than a bra burner. Thomas was able to traffic in Jew hatred by intimidating American men. She shouldered male journalists aside not to break the glass ceiling but so she could intimidate presidents.

Helen the Hideous had nothing on Bellicose Bella. Abzug never missed an opportunity to praise murderous regimes while bashing America. She once thundered, "Imperfect though it may be, the Beijing Platform for Action is the strongest statement of consensus on women's equality, empowerment, and justice ever produced by governments." That was in 1995, only seventy-five years after Americans ratified the Nineteenth Amendment, which gave women the right to vote. Meanwhile, China's one-child policy resulted in plenty of girls never being born. It may seem odd for a flaming feminist to support such sexism, but leftists love anything that increases abortions. She pushed gay rights, environmental rights, and racial justice, all of which have nothing to do with improving the lives of women. Abzug convinced a whole generation of women that feminism required leftist activism. Her husband was a member of the Young Communist League, and she shared his leanings in practice if not in title.

She was also a typical leftist hypocrite. While pushing the gay agenda on everyone else, she lamented having two daughters who both turned out to be lesbians—adding fuel to the fire of nurture versus nature. After decades of claptrap about being a strong, independent woman, she confessed her emotional dependence on her husband. She encouraged young girls and women to try to defy biology, all the while pining for her husband's strength and heterosexual children.

Even if you haven't heard of Bella Abzug, you've probably heard of one of her "children," her insidious spawn. Bella Abzug is the mother of the gender-free bathroom madness. Her call for people to reject biology in favor of self-chosen identity is what's behind letting men into girl's bathrooms, as long as the men say that's where they belong. Well, of course they're going to say they belong there. What else would a pervert say?

Bella Abzug couldn't see the madness that would cause— though that wouldn't have stopped the lunatic—which is exactly where we are today: people are so warped that they're willing to give up safety and privacy so that more perverts than transgenders can use any bathroom they want. She didn't think down the road, and as a result her actions, which she thought would protect women, ended up putting them in danger, and the liberals have all embraced her theories.

Like Abzug, Timothy Leary did everything he could to destroy young minds. I knew that clown personally. His drug of choice was LSD. He became an academic who became famous for telling students to "turn on, tune in, drop out." Psychedelic mushrooms were part of his curriculum. His idea of humor was spouting destructive thoughts disguised as harmless platitudes. "There are three side effects of acid: enhanced long-term memory, decreased short-term memory, and I forget the third." Acid does not enhance long-term memory.

Like many typical leftist academics, Leary was as anti-God as he was pro–drug use. He said, "Monotheism is the primitive religion which centers human consciousness on Hive Authority. There is One God and His Name is (substitute Hive-Label). If there is only One God then there is no choice, no option, no selection of reality. There is only submission or heresy. The word Islam means 'submission.' The basic posture of Christianity is kneeling. Thy will be done."

Leary influenced a generation of young minds to equate Christians kneeling in prayer with Muslim terrorists. It is no wonder that after the September 11 attacks so many liberals sought to equate a mythical radical Christianity with the truly violent radical Islam. Meanwhile, the CDC reported that an all-time high 47,000 people died from drug overdoses in 2014. The insane liberal response is to push for *more* legalization. Colorado and the state of Washington have turned into drug centrals with a few trees. Young people flock to Denver and Seattle to tune in, turn on, and drop out. If they're lucky, they won't drop dead.

Allen Ginsberg was another leftist who contributed to America's moral decline. He abandoned his Jewish faith to take up Buddhism, yet his real religion was leftism. He was a beat poet, which even today is considered by leftists to be an actual vocation. Beat poets are like community organizers, but with more candles. Ginsberg's famous 1956 poem *Howl* excoriated capitalism and paid glowing tribute to homosexual sex. After being put on trial for possession of stolen goods, he pled insanity and spent several months in a mental institution. In leftist circles, that made him an intellectual.

In the 1950s, publishers refused to print *Howl*, deeming it a work of pornography. When one publishing house did publish it, it was put on trial. The charges were dismissed when an activist judge declared that graphic descriptions of anal sex had "redeeming social importance." Naturally, that made Ginsberg a hero to leftists everywhere. Like Leary, Ginsberg's support of LSD brought him more followers among those seeking to tear down America's fabric.

In 1956, Ginsberg wrote, "America, I used to be a communist when I was a kid. I'm not sorry." Ginsberg found in his travels that other nations were not interested in his message of political and moral decay. In 1965, he was deported from Cuba for publicly protesting the persecution of homosexuals and referring to the murderer Che Guevara as "cute." His most vile contribution to society was being a supporter and member of the North American Man/Boy Love Association. "I'm a member of NAMBLA because I love boys too—everybody does, who has a little humanity." Just to be clear, we're not talking about Spencer Tracy's movie *Boy's Town*, about the benevolent Father Edward J. Flanagan. The words behind the acronym are meant to be taken literally.

At least Ginsberg failed to become an attorney. William Kunstler succeeded. No act of leftist violence was too shameful for him to defend. He was the defense attorney for the Chicago Seven, the anarchists who set Chicago ablaze during the 1968 Democrat Convention. As a result of his advocacy, Jerry Rubin, Abbie Hoffman, Tom Hayden, and the other four miscreants spent zero days in jail and paid zero dollars in fines.

Kunstler also defended the utterly indefensible Weather Underground terrorists. Obama's pal Bill Ayers—the felon who was Obama's mentor, who was front and center in the anti-Trump protests in the spring of 2016—set off bombs that murdered innocent civilians. After Ayers and his wife, Bernardine Dohrn, were acquitted, Ayers chirped, "Guilty as hell, free as a bird." Ayers spent his postterror years influencing a new generation of potential domestic terrorists as a professor. The Weather Underground was a self-described communist revolutionary group seeking to overthrow imperialism.

Kunstler defended the violent militant Black Panther Party. Many of the Black Panthers were eventually convicted of violent crimes, including murder. The globe is still reeling from their brutal activism. Modern groups from the New Black Panther Party to Black Lives Matter have taken part in violence under the cloak of social action. The New Black Panthers held billy clubs outside polling stations in an attempt to prevent white voters from participating in the political process. In Ferguson, Missouri, Baltimore, and elsewhere, Black Lives Matter is known for burning down stores, looting, and stealing electronics in the name of racial justice.

Abzug, Leary, Ginsberg, and Kunstler are not abstract theoretical agitators. Leary hired me to guard his LSD from being stolen. Ginsberg briefly appealed to me. I was a young leftist on the verge of my own insanity. I was naive and stupid. I grew up. They never did.

It takes time to destroy a civilization, and, like ancient Rome, it typically occurs from within. Even the worst activists have to learn their behavior from somewhere. There is no leftist activist gene, unless one believes that babies are born stupid. Miserable ideas have to be taught, and the original teacher of leftist activism was an Italian communist named Antonio Gramsci.

Gramsci's legacy is his theory of cultural hegemony. Gramsci posited that the key to capturing a society was by taking over its cultural institutions. Winning political elections was not enough. Republicans controlled the White House for twenty-eight of the forty years between 1968 and 2008. During that same time, leftists still made advances. Conservatives focused on winning 270 votes in the Electoral College, normally by an Al Gore–proof, William Kunstler–proof majority. Liberals hijacked the cultural institutions.

During World War II, Hollywood was patriotic. Jimmy Stewart was a war hero. Tyrone Power was a marine. Future star Burt Lancaster served in Europe while Charlton Heston was stationed in the Aleutians. Clark Gable trained as an Air Force gunner. Gable was too old to enlist, but he went anyway. Do you understand what America meant to those men? American movies accurately portrayed America as the good guys. Cartoons such as "Der Fuehrer's Face," which featured Donald Duck, mocked Adolf Hitler. Just before the United States entered the war, the great Charlie Chaplin lambasted both Hitler and Benito Mussolini in *The Great Dictator*. That was then. Now? Hollywood is now run by ardent liberals. The few pro-American movies out there have to be privately financed to get made. And when they are, the filmmakers are usually pilloried in the press. Religious movies such as *Ben-Hur* and *The Ten Commandments* used to be mainstream. Everyone went to see them. Now they're a niche market, barely getting a theatrical release before showing up on Netflix.

Look at television. There used to be shows about heroes such as *Gunsmoke* and *Peter Gunn*. There were shows with respected father figures such as *Bonanza* and *Father Knows Best*. In the 1970s, we even had *Good Times*, in which John Amos played a strong black father figure. Then came dad as clown. From *The Cosby Show* to *Everybody Loves Raymond*, the father was reduced to a punch line. On *The Simpsons*, the father is a moron. The mother is the adult, and the father is just another child for the mother to contend with. It is no wonder boys are growing up emasculated. The Left has wiped out the father as a respected figure.

The Left has long owned the big three television networks, but one of them has turned its entire programming into leftist indoctrination. NBC owns more than the communist-leaning MSNBC. The parent company has done plenty of indoctrinating on its own. Climate change used to be the domain of a few crackpots. Now every night kids are bombarded with "The more you know" ads that are far from innocuous. Little kids are scared to death that the Climate Change Bogeyman is hiding under their beds, preparing to leap up and drown them in acid rain.

In 2004, Americans overwhelmingly supported gay marriage bans. Ballot measures defending traditional marriage played a key role in President George W. Bush's reelection. The public supported traditional marriage. Then the television networks intervened. Ordinary people in Middle America were portrayed as outside the mainstream. By the time the Supreme Court legalized gay marriage in June, 2015, the public opinion had already shifted. Young people were almost lockstep in favor of gay marriage. The television carpet bombing of their minds worked. Women kissing women and men with husbands are now standard fare on prime-time television. They appear way out of proportion to their actual presence in our society. In an effort to promote as much contrived, unrealistic, antiwhite, antiheterosexual diversity as possible, those characters are often gay *and* people of color. Don't believe me? On the CW—which caters to a very young demographic—two popular shows are *The Flash* and *Arrow*, both about superheroes. One has a white police captain who mentions his husband more than any other male character talks about a wife. The other has an African American scientist who is always talking about or showing up hand in hand with *his* boyfriend. On that same show, the white female superhero, Black Canary, has a female Asian lover.

While ISIS recruits young killers, we're recruiting our young to the gay lifestyle. The lunatics are running the asylum.

In addition to the entertainment industry, liberals seized control of the schools. Randi Weingarten is the president of the American Federation of Teachers. Her job is to make sure that teachers who molest children are given protection from being fired. Try firing a bad public school teacher. Then wait a few years. The unions give millions of dollars to liberal Democrats in exchange for lifetime protection for all involved. Teachers are free to indoctrinate students without any fear of interference from parents. *Huckleberry Finn* gets removed from classrooms, while *Heather Has Two Mommies* replaces it.

The Left controls the libraries. When was the last time you saw a Republican librarian? Like Facebook, which we now know shuts down conservative-trending topics, the libraries decide what books are on the shelf and what books are restricted.

Facebook does so in part by design and in part out of ignorance—the indoctrinated children who monitor its sites don't recognize topics of interest to conservatives because they weren't exposed to them when they went through their Ivy League towers. A Facebook contractor once admitted that there was bias in what it chose to keep out of the trending topics and that the company's minions were doing so subjectively.

You don't have to delete something in order to censor it; you just have to bump it down in the rankings so nobody can find it. Then the liberals can say, "That's not censorship. We don't censor." No, they don't. They just hide facts they don't like.

Facebook isn't the only institution exercising this sort of suppression. Go to your local library and see how many more copies it has of some liberal diatribe written by Bill Maher or Al Franken than my own books, even something sweet such as *Teddy and Me*, which, as many of you know, is about my dog. And where are those copies, if they do have them? Hidden away from the eyes of the people who most need to see them. People who need to be exposed to new ways of thinking. Sane ways of thinking.

When I was growing up, the most radical music we had was by Chuck Berry and Elvis Presley. Today, music is the domain of the Left. Rappers sing songs about murdering police officers. Then young people march in the streets chanting for more dead officers. When the inevitable happens, the Left expresses shock that their calls for violence lead to violence— then blames the cops anyway. And where is the outrage from feminists when rappers talk about beating women or refer to women as "hos"? I won't ask how an abbreviated version of "whores" became a term of endearment among African Americans. It came from a systemic lack of respect for women. I won't even ask how the progressives failed to call the culture out for that: they didn't want to stifle racial expression, except among whites. Or didn't you see the quick demise of the Confederate flag, the de facto ban on whites playing previously white parts in white Broadway shows such as *1776*, the attempt to silence Donald Trump wherever and whenever he spoke?

The lunatics aren't just running the asylum, they're running our nation, ruining our nation.

The Internet is supposed to be free and open for people to seek information as they see fit. Try looking something up. Google it. Google is run by a hard-core leftist. So are YouTube and Facebook. A Freedom of Information Act request led to the release of some of Hillary Clinton's emails. One of those emails showed that her people had sent various emails of their own to executives at Google and YouTube. After the Benghazi debacle, Clinton's people persuaded the executives to block the YouTube video that Obama and Clinton blamed for the attacks. Had Americans seen the actual crudely made video, they would have scoffed at the notion that the attack on Benghazi had been about a video. The video was blocked for several days while the Obama administration had its employees get their lying stories straight.

I mentioned Facebook before. Facebook's founder, Mr. Undershirt, Mark Zuckerberg, is another one who shuts down pages on his site that are critical of Islam. Yet pages dedicated to finishing off the Jews are allowed to stay up. Zuckerberg is an indoctrinated millennial who now uses his multibillion-dollar empire to poison the next generation of young leftists-in-training.

Our schools, libraries, movies, television, music, and social media are all used to advance a politically correct, antiwhite, anti-American agenda. Meanwhile, Islamists use all of these tools to advance teachings of their own physical and moral superiority. When traditionalist Americans flex muscle, our cultural institutions make sure we are derided as imperialist, ethnocentric bigots. When Islamists spew rhetoric that is actually imperialist, ethnocentric bigotry, our cultural institutions tell us to be hypertolerant in the name of diversity and multiculturalism.

Gramsci's teachings gave us Abzug, Leary, Ginsberg, and Kunstler. They taught our children their anti-American, antiheterosexual, antimale, antiwar, radical environmental agenda. The cultural institutions spread the lies. The newest cultural institution, social media, spreads these anti-American messages to every corner of the globe in seconds.

The result is leftist agitators Barack Obama and Hillary Clinton reaching the highest positions of power. Barack Obama didn't start this decline. He was put in place by the radical Left—a cabal of Ted "Liberal Lion" Kennedy, Howard

Dean, John Edwards, and John Kerry—to push it as far as he could. Mao Tse-tung's China is apparently the model.

I am currently reading two gigantic biographies: *Mao: The Unknown Story* and *Wild Swans: Three Daughters of China*, both by Jung Chang. She actually lived through China's Cultural Revolution. She grew up in China's communist elite, was living in a world of privilege, and worked in the Red Guards. Then she turned against the tyranny of Mao. She tells the story of the Cultural Revolution, in which her own parents were denounced, tormented, and sent to labor camps far from the luxuries of the homes that they had known. Her father had stood up to Mao Tse-tung. He was a part of the communist hierarchy, but he eventually had enough with that crazy madman, Mao Tse-tung, and stood up to him. But he was driven insane and hounded to death. Jung Chang was exiled to the edge of the Himalayas as a teenager, and she worked as a peasant and a barefoot doctor.

You think it can't happen here. I'm telling you this because you think that we're immune and that we're protected by a Constitution. Well, there is a man in the White House who shreds the Constitution one page at a time in every way he can. He and his psychotic band of gangsters do everything they can to undermine every amendment to the Constitution. Attorney General Loretta Lynch replaced gunrunner Eric Holder. Lynch has threatened to take away and imprison those of us who engage in any kind of speech that she deems is "edging towards violence" regarding Muslims. She is also looking for ways to prosecute and jail climate change skeptics. Her friends who control the universities are imposing speech codes according to which every boy is a potential rapist and every girl a victim. Social justice has replaced actual justice. Just ask the Duke lacrosse team.

Funded by that criminal agitator George Soros of MoveOn.Org, Obama and Hillary have been grooming the next group of Marxist social justice warriors. Black Lives Matter, Code Pink, Occupy Wall Street, and every other violent leftist group is a direct consequence of Gramsci's model being applied to the most vulnerable among us, our children. Where is Lynch when Black Lives Matter agitators say that privilege can be eliminated if the privileged step aside—or are forced aside—to make room for the so-called less fortunate, or, as I like to call them, the less motivated? Where is the protection for free political speech then? Is that hate speech or protected speech, according to Lynch?

Ask Donald Trump how his free speech is being protected when Black Lives Matter, MoveOn.Org, and other domestic terrorist groups interrupt and suppress his rallies. Lynch likes free speech for just a privileged few children—her favored children. How is free speech being protected when Obama mandates that any company using the words "Negro" and "Oriental" instead of "African American" and "Asian" will henceforth be denied government funds of any kind? How is *anybody* protected when the government edits the phone conversations with the shooter in the Orlando nightclub massacre and takes out references to Islam—references the shooter himself made! They're part of the record! How can it be offensive when a Muslim himself says them? Isn't that what we're always being told—that you can't use those words because they're *our* words? So now they're even censoring Muslims who want to tell the truth about their sick beliefs.

The dictator is rewriting the dictionary. He's rewriting history. Except the bad history he makes. We'll have that forever if Hillary wins.

No, wait. Burning books would produce environmentally damaging smoke. He'll compost them instead.

While our indoctrinated, young, leftist radicals are tearing America down, our Islamist enemies are building their armies up. Our kids are curled up in the fetal position in their safe spaces hiding from climate change monsters. If they are the last line of defense, the Islamists should soon be able to take control of America the way they did Europe. It's time to build an ark, folks. As King Louis XV of France put it, *"Après moi, le déluge"*: though the Caliphate in the Middle East is apparently stillborn, the threat is far from ended.

IS THE USA NOW LIKE THE USSR?

It's hard to get a message out when the media is corrupt.

I saw an article, "Back in the U.S.S.R.? How Today's Russia Is like the Soviet Era." It's a hit piece on Russia. The American dunces who hate America—in other words, the entire press corps—all hate Vladimir Putin, too. The official government press in the United States is ABC, CBS, NBC, CNN, and, by the way, Fox News. You can throw Fox News into the mix of the official government press.

Why do I say that Fox News is now a government mouthpiece? I saw a poll on climate change on the Fox News Channel. I looked carefully. It asked, "Do you think the

United States should sign the climate treaty?" On Fox News they said that 66 percent said yes. Except they were quoting a CBS poll, not one of their own. Now, why would Fox News quote a CBS–*New York Times* poll unless they're part and parcel of the same establishment mentality? The answer is that they wouldn't, unless they are. So now you can put an X through Fox News.

So all the media in America hate Putin, even though he's now revered by most people in the world because he's the only one with the guts to take on ISIS. We have a media that is so corrupt it tries to tear down someone doing good, just because Barry from Honolulu—this thin, smoking, hostile man in the White House—is so jealous, so envious of Putin's strength and resolve and popularity, as any narcissist would be. And it's because Putin isn't an elitist: he didn't go to the best schools, and he doesn't always behave in a way the elite thinks he should behave. He's blunt to the point of crudeness.

By the way, does this sound like anyone who is running for president? That's another reason why Barry doesn't like him.

Most of all, though, it's because Putin and Barry are on opposite sides of the critical issue of what to do about terrorism. If you study world events the way I have done, every day of my life since I was eighteen, you'll see that your president is backing ISIS. Do you have to be a genius to figure that out? All the weapons ISIS uses are US-made weapons that Barry ordered to be left behind.

Not that Barry is alone in his hatred for Putin. Turkey shot down a Russian jet, which by the way was shot down over Syrian airspace, and it landed in Syria. There was no warning given. All of you who supported Turkey should be ashamed of yourselves. You're nothing but holdovers from the Reagan era. You think that this is the same Russia as the Soviet Union that Ronald Reagan hated. You idiots have to grow up! You have to open your mind to what's going on here! Don't you see that you're now on the side of Turkey and the ISIS groups?

Back to the leftists in the media. NBC tries to do a hit piece on Putin. As I mentioned before, It was called "Back in the U.S.S.R.? How Today's Russia Is like the Soviet Era." The diatribe—which also defames a great Beatles song, by the way—lists how they are similar. First, "The Anthem. One of freshly elected Putin's decisions . . . was to restore the Soviet national anthem from 1944—the one he grew up with. Two-thirds of the population approved of the move by 2002."

So that's a bad thing to the communists in this country, or shall I say the new socialists in this country, or shall I say the men without a country in this country? They don't like the Russian anthem. That's a sign that they're living in the Soviet era.

NBC continues, "The Party. In Soviet times, there were no parties other than the Communist Party, and membership was a prerequisite for career advancement." Why don't you just substitute the word "Democratic Party" and tell me if it's any different from America today? Tell me if it's different among the news media today and among the politicians today.

Next it goes to "Spies." Here's what the article says: "By the mid-2000s, up to 80 percent of the Russian ruling establishment was made up of people with backgrounds in security services, according to a study. . . . The trend was confirmed in numerous subsequent studies. Above all, this included the Soviet secret police, the KGB, which handled counter-espionage and brutally suppressed political dissent." Okay, that's real. Now, "The KGB's successor the Federal Security Service"—the FSB, okay? If you watch *Homeland*, that's the FSB—is "both powerful and feared. It is tasked with fighting spies and extremists, but it also monitors the political opposition to the government."

Think about the FBI in America, the CIA in America, the Department of Homeland Security in America. Don't you think they're powerful and feared? Don't you think they're tasked with fighting not only spies and extremists but also the American people themselves? Don't you think those organizations also monitor the political opposition to Obama's socialist government? Of course they do. So what's the difference between the Soviet Union and the United States in this regard? Very little.

Next: "Dissidents." Trying to hit Putin again, the article says, "Joseph Stalin, the Soviet Union's feared leader who ran the country with an iron fist from 1924 to 1953, purged, imprisoned and executed his critics. Even in post-Stalin times, the regime punished those who threatened or disagreed with it so dissidents were fired, jailed, expelled, confined to psychiatric wards and harassed by the KGB."

That's all true. I read my Solzhenitsyn. But what does it have to do with Putin? The Russians don't do that anymore.

The article goes on to say, "Russia's opposition today also fights an asymmetric battle: its leaders face criminal cases and regular arrests, thugs harass them at events and officials drown them in red tape." I said, "Really?" Now let's look at America. Let's see what the opposition to Obama faces. Let's see, do the opponents of Obama face criminal cases? Oh yeah, how about that bakery case? How about all of the people who were punished by the illegal, illegitimate, fascistic IRS or EPA?

Then the article says that in Russia thugs harass opposition leaders at events. Are you telling me that conservatives are not harassed at every event by government thugs or by thugs in America who are working for Black Lives Matter, the National Action Network under Al Sharpton, or Jesse Jackson's thugs? Are you telling me that they're not thugs who are fundamentally working with and for the government? The article finishes by saying "and officials drown their opponents in red tape." Oh really? The IRS and the EPA don't do that in our country?

Okay, let's go down the list. This is a very important thing for you to understand. NBC, in its attempt to continue to smear Putin, tries to demonstrate that Russia is like the Soviet Union, but the network can't do it. Moreover, everything it says about Russia actually applies to America under Obama.

I'll include another one. "Media Control. Soviet media broadcast only what officials wanted it to, and access to foreign media was banned. In the 2000s, one of Putin's first moves was to bring back under state control the leading television channels, Russia's main source of information. They have since turned into pro-government vehicles."

I'm going to ask you straight out: Are you telling me that our liberal media is not exactly like state-controlled media?

Tell me how they differ! Tell me they're not progovernment vehicles.

Then NBC goes on and undermines its own argument when it says, "Nevertheless, Russia has many independent small media outlets that offer alternative points of view. Now because of the Internet, cable, and the accessibility of international print media, Russians can get their hands on a wide variety of organizations." So what's the point? There is no overt media control as there was in the Soviet Union.

Now we get down to the meat of what they're really getting to here. Go to the bottom of this hit piece, and you'll find the mother of all lies. "Homophobia. In Soviet times, 'sodomy' was punished with up to five years in prison. In Putin's Russia, 'promotion of homosexuality' to minors carries fines and arrests, and public displays of same-sex affection or transgender behavior can result in public abuse." Now the article contradicts itself: "But homosexuality is not a crime anymore, even if some people are intolerant of it and public figures often speak out against it."

Ladies and gentlemen, I rest my case. The fact of the matter is that you know and I know there are no dangers for people of different sexual orientations in Russia. You know that as well as I. But you also know that there's a war against Putin for a number of reasons. And one of the reasons is that he's doing the one thing the Obama administration can't stand: at home and abroad, he's winning.

3

OUR INTERNAL ENEMIES

OBAMA IS INVADING HIS OWN NATION

The people in this country have followed the leader, only it's no children's game. He's leading us right off a cliff.

Make no mistake: This leader is extremely powerful. His will is one of the most powerful I've seen in my lifetime. Barack Hussein Obama, a president who was never touched personally by oppression, has one of the strongest wills I've ever seen, similar to those of other very dangerous leaders. Look at Germany, at Belgium, at America, at the guilt-edged humanitarian rush to bring in Syrian Muslims and Bosnian Muslims. No one knows who they are or where they're really coming from. Ninety percent of them are men without women and children. Of course, the news media are modifying that reality to suit their liberal agenda. They are showing us pictures of older men, frightened women, and hungry children. But we all know that the influx to Europe is 85 to 90 percent single men of military age.

I had a thought about Angela Merkel, the German Dark Angel who is ushering in a new Dark Ages. I thought about her, and a vision came to me. Maybe it's a nightmare; it's tough to tell them apart these days. Hitler invaded other countries to take their territory, to dominate other countries with Germanic people and with the crazed mentality of the Nazi philosophy. In a perverse left-wing repudiation of that, Merkel is invading *her own country*. But don't be fooled: it's still fascism, the ugly suppression of criticism and opposition by a dictator.

Obama is doing the exact same thing. Obama is invading his own country. He's destroying it from within, like a worm in an apple—or the communist mayor in the Big Apple. He began with illegal aliens from Mexico, Honduras, El Salvador, Guatemala, and China. Using glib lies and illegal executive orders, and unchallenged by the complicit mainstream press, he is making his own people stand down. He's making the local police stand down. He's making the border patrol stand down. There were illegal Mexicans living in a refrigerator box on a hillside in Riverside County, California. The Immigration and Naturalization Service was summoned—and took no action.

"It's a domicile," the agent told a concerned citizen who called, since it was a route frequented by drug mules. "We no longer have the right to enter."

It doesn't matter which way the psychopaths operate: conquering or allowing conquest. It's still psychopathic behavior. You won't read it in the morning newspaper along with a picture of some slut from Hollywood slipping on a banana peel on Sunset Boulevard. It's important, but it's not sensational. Do you understand the difference? Tyrants depend on our compliance along with our short memories and even shorter attention spans.

Hitler was a certifiable psychopath. Everybody knows that. He used force, violence, and fear to expand his nation. He invaded other countries. He exterminated entire populations.

What does Merkel do? What is Obama doing? He invades his own country with a de facto army from other nations, foreigners who are not even citizens, who have no visas or legal right to be here. He wipes away the laws of his own land. He permits illegal aliens to vote. If that's not psychopathic behavior, tell me what is. In July, 2016, an Afghan refugee affiliated with ISIS attacked train passengers in Germany with an ax. Police shot him dead. That's just the beginning!

Why are these leaders behaving this way? We'll get to that in a moment.

I got an email from someone who's far smarter than I am. It's not easy for me to say that because I believe in myself. But I do know a few people who are smarter than me, particularly one who has a remarkable capacity to extrapolate, to look ahead.

"It's over," he said to me. "What Merkel is doing to Germany, what the weaklings are doing to England, what the socialist is doing to France, what Obama the psychopath is doing to America: all of this will render those countries nonexistent in less than fifty years."

I replied, "Maybe you're right, maybe you're wrong."

Here's a phrase for you: *blunted optimism*. That's what I felt then, and I feel it even more now. The inescapable fact of the matter is that the world is changing in ways we could never imagine.

Does anybody else on Earth see this the way I do? Maybe, maybe not. But I will continue to try to awaken you. I have been sounding the clarion call for years. The problem is, it's very late in the cycle. We may have already lost the battle. Do you understand that? Let me repeat: we may have lost the battle. All you can do now is prepare for the tsunami of foreigners, of illegal aliens, of those opposed to Christianity and Judaism that the psychopaths are allowing—no, encouraging—to rush across the borders as quickly as they can.

If there is any hope at all it's that a popular uprising can at least slow down the damage. When the United Kingdom voted to exit the European Union, the British people taught us what can happen when people who love their country stand up against waves of immigrants. And though I'm not a fan of the British bureaucracy—the one that banned me, not terrorists, from ever entering their nation—the people deserve my support, our support.

So returning to the question I posed above: Why are world leaders behaving that way, from Barack Hussein Obama to the ballet dancer running Canada to every Western leader not named Putin or Castro or Mexico's president, Enrique Peña Nieto, who gives us the people he doesn't want?

The answer is frighteningly simple. Two of the hallmarks of the psychotic are egotism and the need to destroy. It is the goal of these dictators to make certain that traditional Americans (and Germans and Englishmen) in general, and the white male in particular, no longer have a voice in their own nation. They are the enemy, and they are within.

It is our job to stop them.

THE MOST DANGEROUS SUBVERSIVE ORGANIZATIONS IN THE UNITED STATES

Corruption runs deep in the US government, and it will remain there even if Donald Trump wins the presidency. Why? Because the people Obama has put into place are going to still be there.

Let's say Trump wins, and let's say he follows through on 80 percent of what he promises. Take a look at the people Obama has planted in high positions: you can't get them out except by executive decree.

I'll give you one example of a guy we can get rid of, a former assistant attorney general for the Civil Rights Division of the U.S. Department of Justice. A man named Thomas Perez, one of the most fanatical leftists in the history of the world. He was put in there by Barry Obama as a virtual poison pill. Nearly everything is a civil rights violation to this agitator, so he has put in laws and restrictions to make businesses almost inoperable. He'd still be in there, destroying the middle class, if Barry hadn't made him secretary of labor. So Barry did Trump's work for him, because when Barry is out of power, Perez will be out of power, too.

But that's only one person, and there are many other hateful parasites like him infesting the body politic. Want another? Take the former head of the National Council of La Raza, a woman by the name of Cecilia Muñoz, one of the most radical individuals in American political history, who is now sitting inside the Oval Office as a special adviser to Barry. She was moved in there from her post as the White House director of Intergovernmental Affairs. She did such a good job undermining America that Barry rewarded her by bringing her into the Oval Office itself. This is how far the boll weevils have gone. This is how far this government has been penetrated. Fortunately, come January 20, she too will be gone.

How are we going to get rid of the countless other bureaucrats like those two vermin who are now running the federal government even if Trump wins?

*　*　*

You want another one, someone whose influence is not so easily gotten rid of? Jimmy Carter, our former, failed president, who has been a lifetime subversive. He's an all-around scorpion of an individual who spent millions of dollars on public relations in order to make us think he's a kindly grandfatherly guy. I don't see him as that. When Hugo Chávez the dictator was running Venezuela, it was Jimmy Carter who went there to certify his election and stamp it as legitimate when we all knew it was a rigged election.

Have the folks at the Carter Center done and are they doing any further damage here to the American way? Well, Jimmy Carter is a lifelong Israel hater. That we know; that's his stock in trade. He's gotten very far with that. I guess it would be a legitimate question to see what money he's getting from a named terrorist group if, in fact, that turns out to be the case. Is he receiving money from Hamas or Hezbollah through a third party?

We can't, not without changing the system—which I hope a President Trump will do. You can bet a President Hillary will not.

I could go a step further. Take some leftist organizations that have incredible influence and have pulled our country toward extreme liberal socialism. The American Civil Liberties Union is one group. The Council on American-Islamic Relations is another. The Southern Poverty Law Center is another such group.

There are others among the ten most dangerous leftist extragovernmental organizations that need to be taken down when Donald Trump becomes president. Ten treasonous organizations that continue to damage the American way. Ten anti-American organizations that need to be exposed, their leadership called before Congress, their funding traced to all sources. We need to examine all of them, break them up like the old, festering monopolies they are. Break up these leftist organizations to save America.

The number one public enemy, the head of the serpent, is the ACLU. It must be broken apart. Now, if I say that the way to do it is to start with a HUAC, House Un-American Activities Committee, investigation, I know what's going to happen: the Left will go insane. They'll say, "You're violating our civil rights." They'll say, "You do not have probable cause to bring people in to investigate them." They might be right. But we need to do exactly that for our survival.

Tell me how a society that is open like ours, that is democratic like ours, can survive when enemies of freedom, enemies of democracy are destroying society by using the very freedoms that we have in place because of the Constitution? What would you do? This is the conundrum we are facing. These are probably the most important questions of our time: How can civil liberties be protected? And should civil liberties be put above survival? Because with all due respect to Benjamin Franklin, who said that liberty must be placed higher than security, without security, without survival, what good are civil liberties?

That's the problem. This crusade is going to lead us down roads we may not be comfortable going down, but we must go there.

How can the ACLU, the Southern Poverty Law Center, CAIR, and all the damage they're doing to this country be stopped? These groups must be investigated by the new Congress come 2017. Investigated for subversive activities that undermine the Constitution and the American way.

I know these are very loaded statements that are sure to rattle the nerves of everyone right, left, and center, including libertarians. But I'm going to talk about them, because as far as I'm concerned just getting a new president will be a start, but only a start. If it's the right president, there's some hope. Do you doubt that? Look at what one man has done to this country in only seven years. One man can make a huge difference, especially when he's as anti-American as Obama. One man—or one patriot—can make a huge difference. But he's going to need our help. We're going to have to advise the new president, who, let me say again, I hope will be Donald Trump. I hope it's Trump in a landslide.

When Trump wins, we're going to have our work cut out for us. We're going to have to name those and other organizations we want to have investigated.

Look no further than the organizations that have received direct funding and assistance from the mastermind of world disorder, the money changer George Soros and his so-called Open Society Foundations. Here they are: Advancement Project; All of Us or None; Alliance for Justice; America Coming Together; America Votes; America's Voice; American Bar Association Commission on Immigration; American Bridge 21st Century; ACLU; American Constitution Society for Law and Policy; American Family Voices. I can name many more of them, but they're all the same wolf in different sheepskins. Let's bring them into the light and expose them, make them scatter like cockroaches when you turn on the light.

The request I'm making is this: name subversive organizations, or organizations you consider to be so far off the ideal of the American way that they are in fact subversive (meaning that they spend all of their resources going against the wishes of the taxpayer). That broadens it quite a bit, doesn't it? Name those, read about them, and get vocal about them. Get angry about them.

How will you know them?

If being subversive means going against the wishes of the taxpayers, what do the taxpayers want? Does the average taxpayer want more immigrants or fewer immigrants? You know the answer. Most want no immigrants. You have groups that are working around the clock to bring in floods upon floods of immigrants, a virtual tsunami, an indigestible amount, or number, of refugees, immigrants, whatever you want to call them, especially from third-world nations that hate us. These low, unscrupulous organizations are bringing in people who will never, ever integrate into the society, who will spend their every waking minute hating the society, many of whom will go off like rockets. Those groups would be at the top of my list.

As I've said many times for many years, at the top of my list is the ACLU. Of course, its officers will argue, "We're not subversive, we're not anti-American. We just believe in immigration."

Sure it does, as long as it allows foreigners to sidestep borders, language, and culture with impunity. I'd like it to answer some of my questions. For example: "Where do you get your funding from? How much of your funding comes from foreign governments? How much has the Mexican government contributed through front groups?"

There are other organizations. If you want to call them subversive, that's a loaded term, but it's fine, because some *are* outright subversive. The rogue financier Soros spends all of his money on subversive elements in this country. How else would you explain a man who funds organizations that work to flood the United States with Muslim men of military age from Syria and call anyone who opposes them racist? Would you say that's healthy for the nation? Tell that to the women who were raped and robbed in Germany on New Year's Eve 2016. Or flood the United States with Central Americans infected with tuberculosis, Zika, and measles, to name only a few of the newly resurgent diseases they are bringing with them?

Which organizations do you think are dangerous for the survival of America? Who has done the most damage to the American way? Which organizations need to be investigated by the new government in 2017? These are important questions that need to be asked right now. We need to plan ahead, and we need to get them in our sights. We need to start collecting dossiers on the individuals who run them. We need to start getting their names and the names of their organizations, and get them into the hands of Donald Trump's campaign managers as soon as possible, so when he is elected, and when he is inaugurated, on day one he can go after these subversive organizations in order to stop the downward spiral of the United States of America.

That's my speech. That's what I truly believe from the bottom of my heart. But we could say all the things we want from today until kingdom come; it's not going to make one bit of difference. Lawyers have twisted the laws so that you can't even defend yourself against them. That's another thing that needs to be looked at: the American Bar Association itself is a subversive organization. Look at what it has done, who it protects, and who it prosecutes—often pro bono, at no charge.

Will anything come of this? I don't know. I have no idea where it can go. I don't know if Donald Trump is going to win. Those of you who read this book after the election already know the answer to that. All I do know now is that none of the other candidates is capable of going after these organizations. That, my friends, is why Trump is so hated by the far Left and why the media keep smearing him. They know the people around Trump will go after them for what they have done to this country. They know their funding will be cut off and, worse yet, that some of them may actually be indicted for crimes against laws on the books right now.

The *Washington Times* disclosed that George Soros gave Black Lives Matter more than $30 million! He's one of the chief funders of this organization, which does everything it can to disrupt and undermine American society under the guise that all black people are victims. Its false narrative has led to the killing of police and the inability of police to do their jobs to protect us from the stalking wolves. I don't know if you can declare Planned Parenthood to be a subversive group. I would say it's an evil group. Any group that basically is in the business of selling baby body parts is a very evil group. I think this threat could be handled very easily with a new Congress, by having the organization's funding cut off completely. I don't even think you have to investigate Planned Parenthood. You can just cut it off at the funding level, and it'll be out of business before long. I wouldn't even waste any money investigating it; I would just defund it, and that will be the end of it. That's like defanging a snake.

I'm the architect of the new America. I'm a leader in thinking. You know that. When Trump wins in a landslide and the new government takes power in 2017, we're going to be faced with a huge problem, which is all of the boll weevils that Obama has planted like poison pills throughout the federal government. Then, of course, we have the organizations that we know are subversive. I've named some of them. Which organizations do you think need to be investigated by congressional committees when the new Congress convenes and taken down, taken apart, and defunded?

More than that, if there is evidence of criminal activity along the way, punish them for what they have done, are doing, and would do further to damage this nation. There are many organizations whose every waking moment is about disrupting the social order and attacking white people. You know what I'm talking about. Don't pretend it's not going on, and don't pretend Obama's not funding most of them. He specializes in this. He is their bread and butter. He is diverting billions of dollars to them in order to continue to attack us.

The National Lawyers Guild is one of the most dangerous activist groups in the country. Every one of its members is an enemy of the American way. Every last shyster in the National Lawyers Guild is the type of lawyer that you have come to hate, in plain English. Now, they will tell you they're just for the underdog, they're for the poor immigrant. Well, you know what? That may be so, but I'm for the middle class. I want a lawyers guild for the taxpaying middle class, not a lawyers guild for the subversives who are bringing in refugees, immigrants, whatever you want to call them, by the tens of millions.

If you want to know what this country will look like in ten years if this is not stopped, all you've got to do is look south of the border, then all you've got to do is look at Fallujah, then all you've got to do is look at Somalia, and you'll have some picture of what districts or whole regions of inner cities will look like in this country, unless the subversive groups are exposed and stopped.

Then there's Catholic Charities USA. Most people will ask, "How can you attack a church?" You know the answer to that. Catholic Charities USA is not a church. It uses the word "Catholic" in its name, but it has as much to do with Catholicism as the moon does. Catholic Charities USA is a nonprofit organization that uses the handle of Catholicism to subvert US immigration laws. It has, it does, and it will continue to flood the United States with illegal aliens.

All of these groups use the same scheme. These entities with church-related names are 501(c)(3) organizations that need to be investigated and stopped along with the others that we're talking about.

Now, what do I mean by harm to the country? There's an interesting question. People will say, "Well, they're just liberals, they're pushing the liberal philosophy. You're a conservative, you like conservative ideas." Okay, that would be a fair statement, but when you are using your organization to go against the will of the people and to go against the voters themselves, to go against honored national traditions, which these organizations do, then they are, my friends, subversive in the sense that they are subverting the will of the majority of the American people. You cannot disagree with my logic: it is sound. It doesn't matter whether you agree with Catholic Charities USA or the ACLU or the American Bar Association or the National Lawyers Guild. What matters is that what they are doing goes against the wishes of the majority of voters in this country. That's why they have to be investigated and defunded and, if any criminal acts are found to have been conducted, prosecuted to the full extent of the law.

Which brings me back to where I started: the emerging totalitarian Soviet States of America is a result of Barack Obama and the leftist fanatics in the administration like that Iranian-born senior adviser, Valerie Jarrett. Whoever wins the election, at least we'll be rid of that poisonous voice of discontent. You have to look at the subversives in the American Left and what they have done, what they would like to do to this country. In the political sphere right now the clearest exemplar of the radical Left is Barack Obama. He's gotten much further than anyone could ever have imagined he would have in such a short period of time. That's because he's such a silk-smooth salesman for the American Left. But like any salesman, we have to look at what he's selling and at his unscrupulous sales tactics.

And not just him. Bernie Sanders—who ran for the Democrat presidential nomination with the vigor of Trotsky fleeing the Bolsheviks—is an exact picture, a literal stereotype, of the American Left, going back, I would say, to the ILGWU era, that's the International Ladies' Garment Workers' Union. Bernie is a classic low-grade garment workers' union community agitator. You want to look at the American Left, you look into the civil rights movement, the war on poverty, the new Left of each era, the leaders of which have now become great conservatives in their own mind. You'll see there's a Communist Party USA. Its members have disguised themselves now. They're running purely as Democrats. There was the Socialist Labor Party. There were overt Marxist-Leninist groups such as the Freedom Road Socialist Organization, the Progressive Labor Party, the Revolutionary

Communist Party, the Workers World Party. None of them really exists in those forms anymore, because they've been morphed into Barack Obama's administration.

Back then you had Trotskyites who ran things such as the Freedom Socialist Party, Socialist Action, the Socialist Workers Party, Solidarity, the Spartacus League, the Workers International League. They're all small splinter groups right now, because most of the leaders have been absorbed into the current Democrat Party. Then look at the anarchist and anarcho-syndicalist parties in the United States, such as the Green Party. Most of them have become very, very small, because the leadership has been given jobs by MSNBC and other media outlets.

Let's look into this in a little more detail for 2017, because we're going to have a lot of work on our hands to uncouple them from the social and political spheres of influence. Their insidious work began long before the 1960s. We had what we would call socialism in the United States, a socialist type of movement. European socialism was imported into the United States by a Christian sect called the Labadists. In 1683, they set themselves up in a commune west of Philadelphia called Bohemia Manor. Their socialism was religion based, unlike the secular communism of Karl Marx. The Labadists followed the communal practices of the apostles and early Christians.

It wasn't until 1848 that secular socialists hit the shores of America. They were German Marxist immigrants who were fleeing Europe following the 1848 revolutions that swept the continent. Many came to America because our Constitution tolerated their radical ideas. Does that sound familiar?

Now I want to move forward into our century and bring us up to our time so we understand how deeply we have been penetrated by the leftists of the world and what they have done to this country. Many of you feel it, you sense it, but you don't know where it's coming from.

Let's go into the 1960s, the civil rights movement, the war on poverty, and the New Left. You'll find out exactly what they are and what they have done, and exactly what they want to do in the future of the United States of America.

Where shall we begin? Some of these names may be familiar to you, such as Students for a Democratic Society and Tom Hayden. It had activists such as Hayden, who was married to Jane Fonda, as you may remember. Then there were groups such as Marxists, Leninists, and the Progressive Labor Party. In the late 1960s, there emerged the Black Power and the hippie movements. That's possibly where we should begin, because the Black Power movement of today, as exemplified by the Black Lives Matter street thugs, is an offshoot of the early socialist-communist-anarchist movements.

If you don't understand history, you're condemned to repeat it. That's what we're living through right now. What about the hippie movement? Well, I think that speaks for itself. Many ex-hippies are now running the media, running the government, and running academia. Doesn't that tell you all you need to know? Look into that, and you'll see the bridge among anarchism, socialism, Marxism, and progressivism. Bernie Sanders calls himself an independent socialist who was running as a Democrat. He's never really been a Democratic socialist—he has always been a radical fanatic. Always. There are others like him in the government and still others in organizations such as Occupy Wall Street and the rest of the bogus, anarchistic Occupy movement, which are all offshoots of this radical leftism I am talking about.

Okay, so Occupy has fizzled for now. Why am I concerned about this? Because I'm thinking ahead. I'm thinking ahead to when Donald Trump wins in the election come November. Now, some of you may have seen polls saying that Trump has an uphill climb. During the summer, a leftist pollster named Nate Silver, whom I call Nate Sliver or Nate Slither, the darling number cruncher of the Left, said that Hillary Clinton had an 80 percent chance of winning the election.

I laughed when I saw that. Do you know why? Because the bookies in England were giving 80–20 odds on the United Kingdom staying in the European Union. We all know how that turned out, and we all know why. It's the same reason why Trump is going to win here. He is already the overwhelming favorite of that key voting bloc, the independents.

When, God willing, he takes office in January 2017, that's when his work will actually begin, because none of the organizations I mentioned will be gone. In fact, I can guarantee you that their nests are being feathered by the Obama administration as quickly as possible to make certain that they are untouchable, as the Five Families of organized crime once were in the United States of America.

These left-wing groups are far more damaging than any organized criminal organization the nation has ever seen in terms of their damage to the social order. That is a definitive, blanket statement that I can support with pages upon pages of references. Media Matters for America is funded primarily by Soros. It was run in cahoots with John Podesta, Obama's lawyer who founded the Center for American Progress, a liberal think tank in Washington, D.C. Media Matters was closely tied to Hillary Clinton during the period that I was banned in Great Britain, and its fingerprints are all over the smear campaign against me and many others in the conservative movement in the United States. They should be at the top of the list. They're among the evilest anti-Americans in the United States today.

These leftist groups are like a cult, and they feed off one another. I imagine its members sit around smoking pot and drinking wine, and then they start talking to one another with a joke about how they can get over on society, what they can do to disrupt the vote, what they can do to stuff ballot boxes, what they can do to vote ten times, what they can do to have illegal aliens vote, and then they start feeding off one another. One builds upon the other, because no one's ever slapped them down. No one has ever come along and slapped them down for the damage they are doing to this nation.

Some of you may think I've missed the most important of these left-wing organizations. How could we forget that friendly guy Al Sharpton? The name of his group is NAN, National Action Network, and its slogan is "No justice, no peace." How many times has this fine human being, Al Sharpton, been invited into the White House by our even finer president? Forty? Fifty? Something like that. Has the White House released the visitor records yet? What damage has this organization done to America? It was reported that Al Sharpton, a street agitator, pushed for Loretta Lynch to become our attorney general! This is how deep these people go in their damage to the social order of this country. Unless they are turned back in 2017, there is no hope for this nation.

So I'm looking ahead, and I'm telling you what needs to be done.

As a man who has been blacklisted by both the British government and Fox News, I know something about blacklists. That's something the American Left has not experienced in fifty years; being on a blacklist. There are groups that need to be investigated for the damage they have done, are doing, and will do, unless they are stopped by a new Congress in 2017. Let's name some of the organizations that I consider to be very, very left wing and worthy of investigation:

Alliance for Democracy; Amnesty International; Black Lives Matter; Center for American Progress; Center for Media and Democracy; Center for Science and the Public Interest; Citizens for Responsibility and Ethics in Washington; Citizen Action; Citizens Fund, ColorOfChange.org; Common Assets Defense Fund; Cordoba Initiative; Media Matters for America; MoveOn.Org; ProPublica (funded by Soros); Netroots Nation; Tide Center; Tide Center Projects; Tides Foundation; Transnational Resource and Action Center; Turning Point Project; Youth Empowerment Center.

Those are just some. You might also include the Service Employees International Union (SEIU) as a subversive organization. But maybe not: the president of that organization, that big union that gave us California governor Jerry Brown, said she was shocked that 64 percent of her membership is interested in voting for Donald Trump. Don't assume that the organizations they control are composed of members who also want to undo the American way. How about when we look into the American religious Left and its funders? This gets very interesting. It's like a spiderweb: Rockefeller Brothers Fund; Lilly Endowment; the Bain Foundation; Ford Foundation; Rockefeller Foundation; Blue Moon Fund; Joyce Foundation; HKH Foundation; Dolan Charitable Trust; Vanguard Foundation; Archer Foundation; Saul Alinsky's Back of the Yards Community Council; National Hip Hop Political Convention; Cuban Council of Churches; Pastors for Peace; Progressive Religious Partnership; People for the American Way; Interfaith Alliance; Interfaith Worker Justice; American Friends Service Committee; Clergy Leadership Network; America Coming Together; National Council of Churches; Interfaith Center on Corporate Responsibility.

There we have a little sketch of the radical American Left to explain how we got where we are and who the head of the snake is. The head of the snake is enjoying himself in the White House. They are all the grassroots groups that have worked for many years to give us what we now have, which is a debased military and a debased America. And the best is yet to come, according to the leader of the free world, Barack Obama, who said in his January 14, 2016, State of the Union address that he would squeeze the last drop out of the year to make all the changes he possibly can.

I think you get the drift.

The question is, as I've said, can we the people speak out against it loud enough and soon enough? The fate of America lies in your answer.

HOLLYWOOD FOUGHT FASCISM;
NOW IT MUST FIGHT ISLAMOFASCISM

I told you earlier that Muslims are invading Europe.

They're invading here, too. The Obama administration has created an open-door policy for our enemies. Remember how in 2015 an ISIS jihadi attacked a reserve center in Chattanooga, Tennessee, killing four marines? Since then, there have been numerous attacks on these shores and dozens that were caught before they became operational. Many of them were ignored by the mainstream press, such as the FBI agent who was attacked by a knife-wielding jihadi in New York or the thirty Muslims who were caught before they could launch a terror attack on July 4.

But I want to talk about Europe first, since it is being drowned by immigrants as well as the rapidly increasing Muslim populations of segregated, secretive communities. It's the first step of a calculated plan to annex the West, convert it to sharia law, put women into burkas, mutilate young girls, take over the military, force everyone to bow to Mecca, and make Christians pay a tax for being Christian. God knows what they plan to do to the Jews. We have already seen what happens to those who dare to mock Muhammad in France, in Denmark, and in the United States. And we know what could happen to those of us who are trying to warn you.

Ever wonder why are there so many young men coming west but so few women or children? It's because of *hijrah*, which Muslims describe as "*jihad* through migration." Who are the traveling jihadists? They're not all from Syria. Many of them are from Bosnia. Some of them are from other nations.

It really doesn't matter where they're coming from. What matters is where they're going.

Germany, for example.

How did it happen that a nation with a strong conservative bent was suddenly overrun in the opposite direction? Well, you can thank those within its government who are "liberalizing" its immigration policies and in the process are destroying it.

Who is Angela Merkel, Germany's chancellor? What do the traveling jihadists have on her? How did Merkel become a dictator with the power to destroy her own country? For that matter, who gave Obama the power to be God almighty?

As I explained, we know *what* is empowering these evil people; their arrogance and a narcissistic need to tear down anything they didn't build. But *who* is empowering them?

I will use that word until the world hears me: evil. Evil exists. Evil is a leader that does not respect the wishes of the people— other than a small, loud, self-delusional population of like-minded psychotics. The rest of us have a right to our own national identity. We the people have a right to secure our borders, just as we have a right to secure the doors and windows of our houses.

Inherent in our Constitution, in the Bill of Rights, is our right to resist illegal search and seizure. The government has no right to break into your car without a warrant, to break into your house without a warrant. You're protected there. So what gives Mexicans the right to break into your country? Who gives Muslims the right to break into Germany, which has similar protections in place?

Criminals do. Evil political criminals. Merkel may as well have a black burglar's mask over her face and a tire iron in her hands as she breaks the windows of Germany and pries the doors off their hinges.

Don't confuse the issue, as liberals do, by talking about the Holocaust and applying it to these so-called refugees. Stop with the false humanitarianism about how you stand up for something. The truth is, liberals hate those of us who want to preserve our borders, language, and culture, but they don't hate the real enemies.

Hate them. Don't hate us. We're actually your best friends. We are the only ones who are warning America and Europe what these burglars called "leaders" are doing to their own nation. Hate those who have the power to fight *hijrah* and don't use it.

For the rest of us, the question remains how to stop them.

Here's one suggestion. The entertainment community is brilliant, powerful, and pervasive. In another time, when this nation was threatened by fascism, it used all of its powers to ridicule the enemy. Today, this very same entertainment complex ridicules not the enemy but the American people. It ridicules Christians, religious Jews, Republicans, gun owners, police, and those who care about the unborn. If the same entertainment complex were to ridicule ISIS and radical Islam, we would have a great ally in this battle of battles—this battle for the survival of civilization as we know it.

That is what is missing in the battle against radical Islam. The entertainment industry that once fought Hitler, Tojo, and Mussolini, that helped boost morale and focus energy on winning World War II, that rallied Americans around a noble cause, is now a propaganda tool of the Left. During World

War II, in cartoons the Germans were drawn in a certain harsh way to make them look ugly. The Japanese were pictured with buckteeth to make them repellent. Through today's eyes, it's repugnant, but through the eyes of people fighting fascists, it was war. And all was fair.

Today? If you draw the Prophet, you and everyone who works with you is shot. And the leaders imply, "Well, they brought it on themselves, they shouldn't have done that."

The enemy creates ugly pictures of Jews. Have you seen the images of Jews painted by Arabs in the Palestinian territories? Or have they not made it to your local newspaper? Have you seen the propaganda against Americans being promulgated around the world? The enemy is painting you as oafs and idiots, drug addicts, sex addicts, and it is undermining the core of this country.

We need to encourage the synagogue jesters—Jewish leaders in Hollywood who have ceded the moral high ground they previously held—and others in the entertainment industry to cease putting out propaganda before it's too late. By that I mean stopping the propaganda against Christians, stopping the propaganda against the family, and stopping the propaganda against the military and police. Jesters, stop the damn propaganda you're pumping out against everything decent in this nation. Those who sow the wind shall reap the whirlwind. I warn all of you, your day will come. The people know who you are. If you think you can escape forever, you are wrong.

This country is melting down rapidly, and no one knows what will come tomorrow. The people are ready to blow like a pressurized well and spew black oil revulsion at cultural sickness across the plains. The people can't take another day of the filth put out by Hollywood and New York. They can't take another minute of *Saturday Night Live* mocking everything decent and supporting everything evil. They can't take it anymore. Their guts are in turmoil. They are ready to vomit out this filth.

I have spent twenty-two years trying to warn you about these days, these days that we're living in now—twenty-two years. God has brought me to this place, to this day, for this message. Go ahead and mock it if you want. But you know in your hearts that I'm telling you the truth. You know what's coming.

Hijrah.

HOW TO IDENTIFY PSEUDO-CONSERVATIVE BULLIES

I remember when I first heard the word "conservative" floating around in this country. It was during the Nixon years. I was in my thirties. People were saying, "I'm a conservative," and I automatically hated them. Why? Because what came out of their mouths defined them, to me, as rigid, moronic people who wanted to bully me and tell me how to live.

Once again, I was a prophet—like the Ancient Mariner but without the dead albatross. Whether you like it or not, that is how most people in this country see conservatives today. They see conservatives as bullies who push crosses in other people's faces and tell them who to sleep with, who not to sleep with, tell others they're morally superior.

That perception of what are now called "staunch conservatives" is drilled into young minds by liberals in the school system, in movies, and on television. Just think about how conservatives are portrayed in those media. They are maliciously depicted as not cool, not good-looking, scowling malcontents who frown on everyone else and try to tell people "how things should be." Contrast that with how gays, to name just one group, are heroically depicted.

You've seen political ads in which conservatives are portrayed as literally wanting to kill your relatives. Do you remember that ad in which a grandma in a wheelchair was pushed over a cliff? How about the one in which a man said Mitt Romney was responsible for his wife dying? That is how liberals portray conservatives in every conceivable space, and it works. Unfortunately, this cartoonish perception is the one most people have when they hear the word "conservative."

They have help, unfortunately, from the adenoidal minions on the right, who will tell you that Donald Trump is not a conservative. What god of conservatism gave those Judases the mantle and the crown to make such pronouncements? Who gave anyone the right to say, "Only I am a conservative, and anyone who doesn't follow my way is not a true conservative?" Do they even know what conservative means?

The backlash against this sort of bullying is why Trump is going to win. It's going to help almost as much as the bullying of the Left and the vile, thuggish policies of Obama. Trump is not that kind of bully. He may be arrogant—you don't build a financial empire of billions of dollars without some kind of bloated, Herculean self-confidence—but he's not going to tell you how to live your life. He's not going to hit you over the head with a cross or thump you with a Bible.

I have a very strict firewall between the concept of preserving borders, language, and culture and the sickness of racism or telling people how to live their lives. Unfortunately, many conservatives are low-information voters as well. They scream and rant on blogs against anyone who doesn't say the right things. They think that limitation makes them intellectuals. They are the minions the community organizers on the right are now using to tell you that Trump is not a conservative or Michael Savage is not a conservative or this one or that one is not a conservative. They'd be shocked to find out in how many ways Richard Nixon and Ronald Reagan were not "true" conservatives. Does anybody remember that Reagan was a union leader—of the Screen Actors Guild—before he was a politician? You don't think some of those ideas stayed with him into the presidency?

Whenever I hear people pointing fingers and saying "You're not a real conservative, he's not a real conservative; only I know what a real conservative is," I'm reminded of communist organizers in the Soviet Union. They also wanted a purity test. They also drummed people out of their movement who were not pure enough. Did you know that this didactic mentality comes directly from Vladimir Lenin?

What I'm proposing is this: We're living in a constantly evolving world. If you want to be a fanatic and rigidly define conservatism and its principles based on what someone wrote hundreds of years ago, I have a question for you: who alive today obeys your edicts 100 percent?

People like this remind me of preachers who ascend the pulpit with their Bibles, saying "Jesus is going to punish you! Many of you don't believe, but if you do believe, God will come down and save you tonight!" Then, the next day, they're seen with a boy in a car outside the church. Who will save that little boy from them? Other conservatives? Men who have their own flaws and corruption? Fear those who make themselves out to be holier than thou.

I'm warning you to watch out for fanatics on both sides of the aisle. They've called me a chameleon for not rigidly adhering to the didactic definition of what a conservative is. But that doesn't make me a chameleon. My beliefs are very strong, but they're also very forgiving and inclusive. Anyone can believe in borders, language, and culture. Any American would support them. That's why I told you in my last book that a nationalist party would attract millions of liberals, as well as conservatives. And Donald Trump is a nationalist. I was right, because the GOP is his party now. Efforts will be made to steal it from him, to shove the party back into a dark, unenlightened corner, but it will fail. The GOP has changed forever.

The Senate-Democrat-Islamist-Socialist Party blocked the Syrian Refugee Bill. It was a Republican bill to curb the flow of Syrian and Iraqi refugees into the United States in order to prevent terrorists from slipping in. The Democrats said they wouldn't even discuss it. Democrats such as Dianne Feinstein, whose friends and associates must profit somehow from the refugee flow, wouldn't even allow the bill to come to an up or down vote.

President Maobama said he'd veto the bill if it made it to his desk. That's because he wants a flood of refugees to come into America. They are the living personification of his orientation, his proclivities, and his friendships. But do people care? You know the answer. You see it every time an Islamofascist kills innocent people in the workplace, at a train station, at a restaurant, at a fireworks display in Nice. The Left lectures us to go along and get along while the Right spouts warnings, then slips into a stupor with their mouths full of hamburger and beer, like former Speaker of the House John "Tipsy" Boehner.

Do their extreme definitions help you define who you are? Or are you going to insist on excluding anyone who opposes the Democrats on this and says those people are not your allies? Trump's not your ally because he's not pure enough on other issues? Does that mean you'd rather have another Democrat win the presidency, because you're such a fanatical believer in your view of what a conservative should be as opposed to what a conservative needs to be? You lost in the bare-knuckle game of national politics, and now you're in a bad mood? Grow up. Go vote for Grandma Clinton, and see how conservative her administration is.

It's instructive but ultimately unavailing to quote a textbook on what a conservative is. Edmund Burke has been dead for two hundred years. We have to live as conservatives in the twenty-first century. I am a true conservative who understands what is the same and what is different about being a conservative in this century. "Borders, language, and culture" has been my motto since I started in radio in 1994. It has been the essence of conservatism throughout British and American history.

What is different is the means needed to conserve our borders, language, and culture amid the challenges they face today, in the real world, a world in which they are under attack by both atheistic socialist progressives and theocratic Islamofascists, who are ninth-century throwbacks. Policies that Burke or even William F. Buckley, Jr., proposed have nothing to do with the threats conservatives face today.

I am a true conservative who hopes to help you define who you are.

CORRUPTION FESTERS IN BOTH PARTIES

The world is falling apart because new world order universalists such as Barry Obama, Germany's Angela Merkel, and the United Nations have been flooding the civilized world with unvetted Muslims. No one even talks about the rape epidemic anymore. In Germany, if German men stand up and defend their fellow citizens, they're attacked by the police. The police in Germany, who should be attacking migrants and throwing them out of the country, are attacking the nationalists who are trying to protect their women and children.

The very same dynamic is playing out in the United States of America. It's just in an earlier stage. There are millions of men who would like to rise up in this country and protect this nation.

In January, Obama freed an al-Qaeda explosives expert from Gitmo. Did you hear what I just told you? He gave a bomb maker *back* to the terrorists. Obama is acting like a rogue president, a criminal president. Hillary Clinton had an email scandal that would have resulted in the indictment and imprisonment of anyone else. General David Petraeus was broken for doing less. But nothing happens to her. The only explanation is that the retrovirus of corruption which invaded this nation has reached a critical mass.

The fundamental problem, as I see it, is that many people of the 1960s were free spirits. And many of them got stuck in that head space, as they used to call it. They're like bugs that fell into resin and became frozen in time. They still espouse 1960s philosophy, the same mantras that were placed in their heads by the communists of the 1930s who ran the hippie movement of the 1960s. They never evolved, and they don't even understand that they have destroyed their own lives and their own nation.

There are millions of people like that. They are all over Hollywood, and in the universities, unable to move on, unable to evolve, unable to see what they're doing to this nation. They take their marching orders directly from the White House without even knowing it. That's how evil and dangerous this retrovirus is.

We are living in very strange times—the cheeseheads versus the knockwurstheads. Members of one party wear blocks of cheese on their heads, members of the other party wear knockwursts on their heads. The corruption on both sides is equivalent, and the people who represent both sides are equivalent. There is almost no difference in the corruption and the hypocrisy of either side, which is why a true independent such as myself is misunderstood, reviled, and distrusted by both sides. The cheeseheads and the knockwurstheads don't own me, they can't make any money with me, and they cannot control me, so I'm a threat to them.

If you think back to the Reagan administration, many of you think Ronald Reagan was as clean as the driven snow and there was no corruption. Well, there was corruption. His attorney general, Edwin Meese, was the most corrupt attorney general until the first one we had under Obama. The only difference is that Eric Holder, Obama's first attorney general, was ideologically corrupt. He was never caught being corrupt for money. Trust me, those types of people are more dangerous than those who do it for money.

But Meese was corrupt, too. Think all the way back to President Reagan's press secretary, Lyn Nofziger. Why am I calling him corrupt? Well, you have to look up the Wedtech scandal, and you have to find out how, through Elizabeth Dole's relationship with Nofziger, Wedtech was given a $32 million contract to produce small engines for the US Army. Wedtech ended up with around $250 million in no-bid contracts, which was a lot of manufacturing money in those days.

During Reagan's second term, Wedtech's crimes kept piling up. Even Edwin Meese couldn't help but get caught up in the scandals. An independent counsel appointed by Congress said he was complicit. Why? Because Meese's close friend had worked as a lobbyist for the company and sought help from Meese on Wedtech contract matters.

Meese was dirty, but his dirty friends in the administration helped him wash his hands. He resigned in 1988, after the independent counsel wrapped up its investigation. Even though nobody ever brought charges against Meese, the counsel criticized Meese's ethics and other scandalous activities and cronyism perpetrated by the Reagan White House.

Yes, I'm telling you about corruption in the administration of that revered Republican icon.

Read about the Wedtech scandal, and you'll find out that this poison has run through our political system for a very long time. This is why the establishment hates Donald Trump. Is he perfect? No. Will he be a perfect this or a perfect that? No. That's what's freaking them out. They don't know which lobbyist to pay off to reach Donald Trump, and they are panicking because they may have to work for a living.

Compare that with Hillary Clinton, who Trump said "may be the most corrupt person to ever seek the presidency." Take a look at her money sources—if you can find them. I'll tell you who some of them are: they're from front groups for all of those Islamic countries who hate us. Look up her donors, and you'll see.

Here are some more: the Chinese. While she was negotiating policy with China, the Chinese government was paying Bill Clinton to give speeches.

You might say that Donald Trump has also gotten paid for giving speeches, and you'd be right. But there's one difference: Trump wasn't a politician. He didn't get paid for giving speeches while he was in a position to potentially influence policy. Donald Trump is a successful businessman, and people want to hear what he has to say. That's why he got paid to give speeches. But since he added "presidential candidate" to his résumé, he's not getting paid to give speeches.

It's an ongoing war between the good nationalists and the corrupt politicians, between good and evil, between sanity and insanity. It's not too late to stop the bad guys, but time is definitely running out.

DIVERSITY IS DESTROYING DEMOCRACY

Europe has been swamped with Muslim refugees, and some of America's so-called leaders—the misleaders—want to see the same thing happen here. One article after another describes this crisis: "Sweden Close to Collapse," from the Gatestone Institute. "Germany in Grip of Muslim Takeover" from Liberal Forum. You know something's gotten bad when the liberals notice it. Even Reuters—which once decried the term "'terrorist" as "insensitive," if you can believe that—has reported on it.

The people are opposed to what is effectively jihad through overpopulation. It's like a swarm of army ants that moves into some other insect colony and takes over the tunnels. The so-called leadership of these countries is opposing the will of the people and is in favor of eliminating the culture of their countries. Where will it end, and how will it affect us?

Dick "Turban" Durbin is true to his name. He's a Democratic senator from Illinois, and he was given the nickname "Turban Durbin" a long time ago. Turban Durbin has called for 100,000 Syrian refugees to be accepted by the United States of America. You read that right. Not 10,000, as Barack al-Husseiny wanted, but 100,000. Turban Durbin figured he'd raise the stakes.

Why? Because this is the way liberal gangsters work. Raise the stakes. Make it outrageous. If you say it's going to be 100,000, these leftist thugs will settle for 50,000. Whether you think this country should take in more refugees from Syria *at all* is the primary question.

Turban Durbin got his name because he attacked our troops a number of years ago during the war in Afghanistan, comparing them to Nazis. We know he's a fellow traveler with the opposition. There's no question about it. And I don't mean the Muslim opposition. It is Muslims fighting Muslims right now. It is moderate Muslims, such as the king of Jordan and the leader of Egypt, who are fighting the radical insane lunatics. So it's not about Muslims. It's about the fanatics that are being brought in and swept into Europe, hiding under the skirts of the refugees.

That's a separate issue. How many refugees can we take in, especially those who will never ever assimilate into this culture? Not in a thousand years will they assimilate. It's not in their culture to assimilate. That's the way they work. Even British socialists such as Tony Blair had to admit that their idea of "multiculturalism" had resulted in cults that will not become Brits.

This is a tough issue for all of us because we have all been the children of immigrants at a certain point. Everyone in America is an immigrant, including the Native Americans. Yes, they had been here before the so-called white man arrived, and they had been here for a long time. I studied this as a young anthropologist and came to understand the time frame of the Native American peoples—how long they had been here before the colonists arrived from Europe. If you study more deeply and go past the surface in anthropology, you will learn that there are traces of people who were here before the Native Americans. There are skeletons of Caucasian-looking people who were here before the Native Americans. They were thrown out by the Smithsonian Institution because the fact of their existence embarrassed certain individuals. Thrown out faster than that same "museum" wanted to toss the *Enola Gay*, the plane that dropped the first atom bomb, because it might offend the Japanese. You remember, the nation that started the damn war in the Pacific?

Like the army ants I mentioned, the history of life on Earth is about invasion—and human beings are no exception. We're being invaded right now. We're being invaded from the south. We're being invaded from the north, from the east, and from the west. You might say, "Well, that's the way of things," and you might get used to it. They're here, they're near, they're everywhere. The question is, why are liberals so quick to embrace this invasion, and why are traditionalists and conservatives like myself so resistant to erasing the borders, language, and culture of this great nation?

As an immigrant's son, I think about the refugee crisis every day. As an immigrant's son, I have to ask myself, why do I oppose relocating 100,000 Syrian refugees into this country? The embarrassing point is that people will always compare the situation to the Jews and the Holocaust. That is the underlying motif of the entire liberal establishment. The emotional substratum of this entire argument is based upon the Jews in Nazi Germany. And it's a false argument. It's a false one on many levels. I'm sure you can figure out why it's false and why the narrative is being used by those who want to flood the United States with refugees for their own reasons.

Lutheran Family Services is accepting refugees only for the money. It's onboard with Turban Durbin, demanding 100,000 refugees because they make money off of them. They're doing it because they're greedy. They're doing it because they make money off of it. There's a lot of self-interest. There's a lot of greed, and the comparison to the Jews fleeing Germany during the Holocaust is an unsound analogy for a number of reasons. It's not Jews running *from* the gas chambers. This is Muslims running *toward* financial gain—at your expense.

The fact of the matter is that wherever they go—Sweden, Norway, Denmark, Germany—they abuse the social service/welfare systems. How can we take care of refugees when we have so many indigenous poor already? What, is everybody here rich? All of a sudden the country is rolling in money? All of a sudden Obama has cleared everything up and there are no poor in this country who need the help of the government? There's something wrong with this picture.

For many years, I've preached that ultratolerance is killing us. And now we have a brainwashed generation of children raised on Adderall, marijuana, other toxic compounds, with skimpy vegan and other inadequate diets and outright brainwashing in the government schools where they fully believe things that are false as though they are truths. They have no religion but liberalism. They have been taught to live by the Ten Commandments of liberalism:

Man is evil and poisoning the earth.

The earth is a living organism and needs to be protected.

All white people are racist.

All people of color are good.

All refugees should be allowed in and given whatever they request.

If people make too much money, it should be taken from them.

Government handouts have no price tag.

Nature should be protected at all costs, unless you don't like your gender.

Burning the American flag is protected speech.

All players on the international stage have equal credibility.

And so our brainwashed, drugged youth cast their brainwashed, drugged youth votes. We have immigrants who want things for free who are being legitimized in an illegitimate way. Jerry Brown, for example, with his criminal ways, has allowed the Department of Motor Vehicles in California to automatically register illegal aliens so that they guarantee not a one-party system, which is what we already have, but a no-party system—just an autocrat; no party necessary. Just an autocrat in Sacramento, an autocrat in Washington.

This is the dissolution of democracy itself under the guise of diversity. Diversity is destroying democracy.

COMPETITION IS HEALTHY: THE STORY OF MY ALOE PLANT SURROUNDED BY TOMATOES

"The country with the best-educated workforce in the world is gonna win the twenty-first-century economy," says Barry Obama. "I want that to be America."

That must be why he has been bringing in people who don't even have a first-grade education. That makes sense. The best-educated workforce in the world is going to win the twenty-first-century economy, so he keeps on bringing in people, many of whom can't even read or write in Spanish. Then he goes on to push free college their way.

Here's socialism, where everything is free. I would have liked to have gone to college for nothing, too. I had to work. But it didn't hurt me. It gave me life experience, work experience. It made me stronger and made me a better asset to the community and the economy. I learned what it takes to earn for myself and to contribute to society in the process. And I learned that nothing is free. The money has to come from someone's earnings. Giving "free" education to people robs them of all of these lessons and inhibits their personal growth, as well as the growth and prosperity of the society that has to carry them and their lack of understanding for the rest of their lives.

You can learn a lot from a garden. I have a garden on the side of my house where I grow tomatoes. They're planted in late February. Normally they're gone by August, but last year they were still a little green going into September. With such global warming as we supposedly have, they should have ripened in July.

I planted an aloe vera plant in the same garden a few winters ago. It never took off. I placed it toward the back. It didn't like it there. I don't know what it was. It wasn't growing. No matter what I did, it wouldn't grow. It just didn't like it. It looked like it was going to die on me. It was hanging in there, just hanging on, hanging on.

The tomatoes, of course, grow like Jack and the beanstalk in front of and around the aloe, and then behind the aloe comes up basil that I planted years ago. It grew up out of soil again and started smothering the aloe. The other plants blocked every bit of light from that aloe. But in the process, as it was engulfed by the other plants, it started to grow, and soon it was three times taller than before it was surrounded by the competing plants. As the tomatoes and basil engulfed the aloe and competed with it, the aloe vera plant began to get taller and bigger. Why? It's called competition.

That's something Barry Obama—who has been hand carried by others his entire life, straight into the White House—has never learned. You're better off listening to a plant.

4

OUR IGNORANCE
OF HISTORY

THE PALESTINIANS AND HITLER WORKED TOGETHER TO EXTERMINATE JEWS

There was a show on the Military Channel entitled "Nazi Collaborators: The Grand Mufti, AKA Good or Evil," which discussed Muhammad Amin al-Husseini, the Muslim grand mufti of Jerusalem during World War II, and how he collaborated with Hitler, how the Muslims wanted to build gas chambers in the Middle East to exterminate the Jews. This should be a wake-up call to all of the liberals who hate Israel—many of whom say they're not anti-Semitic because they're Jewish themselves yet they're anti-Zionist. What these fools should know is that Husseini wanted to exterminate the Jews in the Middle East before Israel was even created—I'm talking about 1940, '41, '42.

Husseini worked with Hitler, got the plans for gas chambers from the Nazis, and wanted to round up all the Jews in every country in the Middle East and exterminate them.

We keep hearing that the Jews kicked the Palestinians off their own land and that the Palestinians are the underdogs. Those "underdogs" claim that the Jews are evil imperialists who stole the land. I've heard it all. I've analyzed it all. And I'm sure there are some cases of land appropriation being true in the Middle East, in Israel.

But there are many cases of that not being true. In many cases the Arabs gladly sold garbage land to the Jews—garbage, useless, rocky hillsides that they could not cultivate for thousands of years, but that the Jews made flower and grew crops on.

Then, at the same time that Israel was created, the Muslims went on the warpath in northern Africa. Does Libya ring a bell? Algeria? Look at the countries of North Africa. Jewish people lived there for five hundred years. Longer, if you include the centuries when they were in bondage. Guess what your friends the Muslims did to the Jews: they stole their land and kicked them out of the country. Around 700,000 Jews were thrown out of northern Africa. Not only was their land stolen, but also their possessions, their bank accounts, everything. They were driven out.

Where did the Jews go? They went to Israel. It was the only place on Earth that would take them.

Who was the grand mufti of Jerusalem, Husseini? For one, he was a very wealthy man. See, not all Palestinians were poor. He was one of the most powerful and richest men among the rivaling clans in the Ottoman province known as the Judean part of Palestine. But he joined the Muslim Brotherhood in 1928, the year it was created, and he transplanted the Nazi genocide in Europe into the postwar Middle East.

That was before Israel was created. This is for you brainwashed youths who think that the Muslims would be fine if there was no Israel, if only Israel would give up the West Bank and Judea and Samaria. Before Israel was even created, Husseini wanted a Nazi genocide against Jews. In 1929, this wonderful Palestinian went along with the statement "He who kills a Jew is assured a place in the next world."

As a result of that, Arabs went on a rampage throughout Palestine. They killed 133 Jews and wounded 339.

In 1933, Husseini had his first meeting with Nazi consul general Heinrich Wolff in Jerusalem. In 1936, Husseini's incitement led to more rioting in Jaffa. It led to a three-year intifada. In 1937, he met with Adolf Eichmann and Herbert Hagen, who was one of Eichmann's colleagues in the Gestapo's Department for Jewish Affairs. Eichmann ordered that Nazi flags be flown in Palestine and that Palestinians adorn their houses with swastikas and portraits of Hitler. That was before Israel was created.

During World War II, Husseini lived in Berlin, where he traveled in top Nazi circles. He even stayed in Hitler's bunker toward the end of the war.

In 1941, Husseini issued a *fatwa* calling for the Germans to bomb Tel Aviv. At a meeting in Berlin in November 1941, Hitler assured Husseini that his goal was the destruction of Jews—all Jews—living in Arabia.

Hitler provided Husseini with a monthly budget to wage jihad in Palestine. Hitler gave Husseini a radio station where he preached genocide in Arabic. He said this: "According to the Muslim religion, the defense of your life is a duty which can only be fulfilled by annihilating the Jews. This is your best opportunity to get rid of this dirty race which has usurped your rights and brought misfortune and destruction on your countries. Kill the Jews. Burn their property. Destroy their stores. Your sole hope of salvation lies in annihilating the Jews before they annihilate you." That was all before Israel was founded, and it's for all you fools who think that the Palestinians only want the land that was "stolen from them." This is a lesson they don't teach at Harvard.

Near the end of the war, Husseini went on his radio show and preached this, and he was the most powerful Arab at the time. Don't underestimate his influence. He said, "The Versailles Treaty was a disaster for the Germans as well as the Arabs. But the Germans know how to get rid of the Jews. The Germans have never harmed any Muslim, and they are again fighting our common enemy who persecuted Arabs and Muslims. But most of all they have definitely solved the Jewish problem. Arabs," he concluded, "rise as one to protect your sacred rights. Kill the Jews wherever you find them. Allah is with you."

This was also on the Military Channel and it is 100 percent accurate. For two years, beginning at the age of sixteen, around 1945, a terrorist named Yasser Arafat worked for the Mufti, helping to buy and smuggle weapons in the war against Jews. Many reports say that Arafat was Husseini's nephew or cousin.

That genocidal lunatic died in 2004, but the hate spawned by the grand mufti lives on.

So does the desire to build gas chambers.

HOW GUNS SAVED JEWS FROM THE NAZIS, AND WHY THE LEFT WANTS YOURS

There is an article entitled "How Guns Saved 20,000 Jews from Extermination by the Nazis." I would like to share it with liberals who are afraid of guns. Most liberals fear guns, but they should know that during the Holocaust, when 6 million Jews and 8 million to 9 million non-Jews were exterminated by the fascist government of Nazi Germany, groups of Jews who fled into the woods of Belarus used guns.

The most famous group I know of is the Bielski partisan group, the most significant Jewish resistance effort against Nazi Germany during World War II. We hear all the time that the Jews didn't fight back. That's a myth. They did fight back.

They were simple men—not rich men, not elitists. They were local guys living in a village. But after the Germans slaughtered their parents and two brothers in the Nowogródek ghetto in December 1941, three surviving brothers of the Bielski family became great heroes. Tuvia, Asael, and Zus established a partisan group and fled into the Zabielovo and Perelaz forests to save their own lives and those of their immediate family. They formed the nucleus of a partisan detachment consisting at first of only thirty family members and friends.

How did they survive in those woods? In addition to food, they knew they needed guns. How did they get guns? There were no guns allowed in that country at that time, other than shotguns.

They had to either break into farmhouses and steal them or lie in wait for Nazis, and knife them in the neck, and steal their guns. Yes, ordinary men like you and I had to kill in order to live—to kill or be killed. But it was the guns that saved twenty thousand Jews from extermination by the Nazis, not to mention the millions of others who were saved by the guns and bombs of our military, the Russian military, the British military, the Australian military, the New Zealand military, and all the others who fought the scourge of Hitler. It was guns that saved everyone. It was not hot air, and it was not tears. It was certainly not crocodile tears or protest marches.

Those boys, the Bielskis, were just a Jewish farming family living in a village. They knew every tree in the woods, they knew every reed of grass in the swamps, and that helped save them, too. Because they were familiar with the geography, the customs, and the people around them, they were able to elude the German authorities and their Belarussian auxiliaries. With the help of non-Jewish Belarussian friends, they were able to acquire guns, guns, and more guns.

The Bielski partisans later supplemented those arms with captured German weapons, Soviet weapons, and equipment supplied by Soviet partisans, who gave the Jews more guns to fight the Nazis.

There was a movie made about this in 2008 called *Defiance*. Watch this incredible movie to see how they saved twenty thousand Jews from extermination—thanks to guns.

When I hear from a madman like Obama that he believes in the Second Amendment, and he points to a piece of paper, every fiber of my being goes into alarm mode, because I saw Hitler do a similar thing when he came to power and pointed to a piece of paper. I've seen others point to pieces of paper, too. I've never seen a dictator do something illegal that he admitted was illegal. Have you? Have you ever seen a dictator do anything illegal?

It's all in the interpretation, the spin, the sociopathic lie.

For example, when Hitler invaded surrounding nations, he didn't say he was invading them to take anything. He said, "This is a perfectly legal move on the part of the German people to recapture territory that belonged to Germany. We have no intent to harm our friends in Czechoslovakia or Poland. We're simply taking back what is ours. I have it on a piece of paper right here, this was our land."

It's just like the bullies I grew up with in my Queens neighborhood. A bully would never strike a smaller kid without first coming up with a pretext for hitting the smaller kid. He would make up a reason in his sociopathic cowardly mind for attacking the smaller kid. Then he would attack the smaller kid after stating his big lie.

The sociopath in the White House has done the same thing over and over and over again. One lie after another. You or I can't yell "fire" in a theater, but he can yell "fire" in the White House. He can yell "fire" in the White House every day. He can set the nation on fire, pitting black against white, gay against straight, old against young, young against old. Yes, he can set the world afire, pitting Sunni against Shiite, laughing all the way with his sorority around him, his radical wife, Michelle, and his senior adviser without portfolio or legitimacy, Valerie Jarrett.

Does this sociopath also believe in the First Amendment for himself but think that a modest background check should be conducted by his government goons before any of us is able to criticize the government through criticizing him? Try, and you will find out that his government goons have the right to declare you mentally unstable and prevent you from owning a gun. Again, this was something that was done in the Soviet Union. I'm not an alarmist, I'm a realist. It starts with very small steps, smaller steps indeed than you could ever imagine in a nation as polarized as this, with the protections that were built in by men fathoms beyond this little man, protections now being dismembered by this quisling.

What will get us where we need to go is the law, the law, and nothing but the law. This little man from God knows where knows that he has violated the law. He knows that this is illegal, and he knows that a president cannot make law. He knows all of this, as do the Lilliputians around him. Loretta Lynch is a low-grade lawyer from the bowels of the New York court system, handpicked by Al Sharpton, one of the scummiest people on the planet, to be our attorney general. She was never qualified for the position, yet there she sits as though she were a legal expert. Has she ever written a paper that any jurist in the nation would ever quote? No. She's another member of the sorority who now happens to be the number one cop in the United States.

Remember what the number one cop in the United States did almost the first day that she was appointed? She threatened anyone who said anything bad about Muslims. This sociopathic fascistic administration says it believes in the Second Amendment, but that's a lie. After the Orlando shootings, Obama directed his ire at gun ownership. After the attack in Nice, he had nothing to say about rental trucks.

Loretta Lynch said things about the First Amendment that were identical. Identical in tone, identical in her disrespect for the Constitution. On December 4, 2015, our attorney general, *the protector of our laws*, said: "Now, obviously, this is a country that is based on free speech. But when it edges towards violence, when we see the potential for someone to lift . . . lifting that mantle of anti-Muslim rhetoric, or, as we saw after 9/11, violence directed at individuals who may not even be Muslims but may be perceived to be Muslims, and they will suffer just as well, just as much. When we see that, we will take action."

There she is saying she believes in the First Amendment and free speech, but when it edges toward violence, we will take action. Then we heard the same thing from the so-called constitutional lawyer in the White House, another great genius. He knows something about the Constitution. He knows enough about it to go around it. I know other leftists who studied constitutional law, and they did so only to get around it. He says today, "Oh, I believe in the Second Amendment, but we need restrictions on it." I told you he's a sociopath. I told you he wouldn't stop. I pondered in 2015, what might the sociopath do in his last year? Well, now we've seen the sociopath calling for federalizing all local police departments through ACLU (!) oversight! The very same anti-American, anti-Christian, antipolice leftist thugs who now oversee Chicago's police he wants to oversee all police departments.

There were no tears when Kate Steinle was gunned down by an illegal alien in San Francisco. No, he didn't have tears for Kate Steinle, because it's a sanctuary city created by him and his goons. The murder weapon was a gun stolen from a federal agent who never went to jail. The great president didn't even call the Steinle family and offer condolences. And what did he do right after five Dallas police were killed by a black radical? He called for police oversight as he feasted and dined in Poland surrounded by his Eurotrash, one-world, EU buddies. Here is what we must do: we must remember that executive orders can be overridden.

The single best example of executive orders that were overridden by the Supreme Court was that of Harry Truman, who tried to take over a steel plant during a strike in order to control the strikers. The case went to the Supreme Court. The Supreme Court said, "No, no, you can't do that. You can't make law."

Obama knows that. He's an educated man. He went to Harvard. He went to day school in Honolulu, courtesy of his wealthy grandparents. There was no mother, since she ran off with his second Muslim father and ditched her son. That, of course, left him scarred completely with a lot of internal rage, but we won't go into the psychology of the sociopath. We will talk strictly about the issue at hand, which is the mental illness in the White House and where that is leading the rest of us.

We have learned that the sociopathic snake in the White House has hundreds of millions of dollars for background checks for legal gun owners but did not have any such funding for background checks on Muslims of military age coming into this country from Syria, Muslims who are mainly males in their twenties. He had no money to do any background checks on the millions of illegal aliens pouring over the southern border of the United States, nor their health statuses. For the millions of invaders that he pours into America, he didn't have the funds to stop them or to do vetting on them—no money to vet the Syrian Muslim immigrants flooding America. But now, suddenly, he has hundreds of millions of dollars to spend on background checks for legal gun owners. We can all see two and two come together.

Most Americans today have no sense of history. Not only do they not know their own history and could not care less about their own history, but they know less about any other nation's history, which is why Americans today are so vulnerable to manipulation.

Where will America's Bielski partisans get their guns should they need them to defend themselves?

FROM THE ICEMAN TO THE NICE MAN

Headline out of Sweden: a cruise for Swedish high school students on a luxury ship, the MS *Galaxy*. At sea, five Muslims gang-raped an unidentified Swedish woman. When the ship docked in Finland, the Muslims were arrested and went laughing all the way to the politically correct Finnish police station.

Of course, after the Muslim immigrants raped the girl, the Finnish police went to their usual lengths to obscure the identities and nationalities of the suspected perpetrators, just as the American media obscured a photo of the man who shot a police officer in a Virginia bus station in March 2016.

Remember?

There was no picture. We didn't see a picture of James Brown III. See, generally, the only perps who are displayed are those who look like Timothy McVeigh. Those who are descendants of the Iceman. But the Iceman has become a nice man.

I watched a show on the History Channel called *The Vikings*. It is an exception to everything that is wrong with the entertainment industry. I was amazed at the production values. The writing is astounding, the historical accuracy is unbelievable. There was a scene in *The Vikings* worth discussing. I'll summarize it as briefly as I can.

In the scene, a bunch of kids in the Viking village were throwing around some leather-wrapped toy that looked like a ball. There was a little boy in a wagon who was brought out to watch them play. The little boy had been handpicked by his mother, who was married to the Viking chief, to be taught how to be a Viking. He was being taught the old ways of the Viking culture by one of the most ferocious of the Vikings. His mother had begged the ferocious Viking not to let her son forget the Viking ways. The boy's father, you see, had adopted a Christian priest captured during one of their raids on England. At first the Vikings had treated the Christian priest as a slave. But eventually the Christian priest preached Christianity to the Viking chief and in so doing weakened him. He became weak in the eyes of the wife—a Viking woman who wanted her boy to be raised as a Viking, not as a weakling. So she secretly took the boy and told the ferocious Viking, "Raise him as a Viking."

During this scene, the kid was indoors, being taught the Viking ways. Some other little boys were playing outside with the ball. So the Viking warrior who was teaching the kid how to be a Viking took him outside where the ball was being thrown about by laughing boys. And the ball came to the kid in the wagon, and it bounced out of his hand, and the other boys threw it back to the kid. The kid held on to it and one of the other boys ran up to take the ball out of the kid's hands.

The kid grabbed a stick or something, rapped the other boy over the head with it, and killed him. A little three- or four- or five-year-old boy. Just picked up something and smacked the boy in the head and killed him. Broke his head open.

The mother rushed out and held him and said, "Don't worry, don't worry, don't worry, you didn't do anything wrong."

Flash to the end of the show, when there was an interview with the director/writer, who's a genius. He talked about that sequence. And he said, "I wanted to show that the kid was being taught how to be a Viking without a conscience, and they'd done a good job because he hit the boy. He didn't know what he did exactly, there's blood all over the place, and his mother said, 'Don't worry, don't worry, you didn't do anything wrong.'" Meaning they were raising him as a Viking to have no conscience whatsoever. To make certain that he's in the warrior culture.

You understand where I'm going with this? Because I'm about to make a jump. Let's flash forward to ISIS.

They have no conscience. But instead of saying that they are just like the Vikings and they have no conscience, they wrap their no-conscience subhumanity in a religion. Then

they tell you it's the religion mumbo jumbo that directs them
to kill women and children, bury them alive, chop off heads,
set them on fire. Mumbo jumbo, mumbo jumbo. Do you
understand where I'm going with this? From the Iceman to
the nice man.

Now let's go to America. ISIS is training children to
have no conscience, to kill with no conscience, while here in
America we have people screaming about microaggression on
college campuses. We have boys being taught that what they
are thinking is aggressing on minorities in some way. They're
being arrested for thinking about what they want to do with
girls. For being boys.

Tell me who will win this war: the Iceman or the nice
man. Think about it. Think about what I have just written,
because in those few words I have encapsulated for you the
entire battle of civilizations that is going on. I will say right
now that unless this insanity that is coming off the campuses
and out of the psychotic Left is resisted, we are finished. Not
only as a society but as a nation. We will disappear.

But also as a race. Because there is a war against a certain
race right now in America. A black man shoots a cop in the
face, says he hates cops. Immediately the media narrative shifts
to police brutality. The next day there are marches across
America against police. Why? Because black lives matter? You
mean white lives don't matter? Only one race's life matters.
You're not seeing what they're doing to you.

I know this is hard for you to read. I understand that this
is difficult for you to accept. I understand that this is a shock
to the system. But as doctors will tell you, sometimes a caustic

medicine is necessary to cure an illness. And unless all of us resist this insanity—call it whatever you want, liberalism, pacifism, communism, socialism, anarchism, it doesn't matter to me what you call it—it's suicide. That's what it is. It's national, cultural, and racial suicide to put up with this insanity.

When you let 0.5 percent of the population dictate to the rest of the population, the whole population is done. In North Carolina, 0.5 percent of the psychotic population says, "I'm a man today, but I want to go into the women's room, so I'll say I feel like a woman." The governor says, "No, we're not going to permit that." All of a sudden the 0.5 percent of the population goes berserk and calls him a racist, a homophobe, a this-a-phobe, a that-a-phobe, and the governor caves in.

Insanity. Suicide. Cultural insanity. Cultural suicide. The death of a nation, the death of a population. But that's not the only triumph of the nice man over the Iceman. I'm going to talk about Obama boasting about the fact how he has denuked America. He deballed and denuked the military. The military is now passive to the psychotic leftists running the country, where surgery for transgenders will now take priority over combat vets waiting for treatment! What a sane utilization of resources. And, might I ask, why permit transgenders into the military who demand immediate and free surgical realignment of their private parts, expensive hormone treatments, and counseling? How can they serve while recovering from this sexual mutilation? Is this a rational use of resources or the deranged priorities of a madman?

Then he talks about reducing the risk of terrorists getting their hands on nuclear material. How will he do that?

We were told that ISIS is about to set off a dirty bomb by someone in Great Britain, and our peripatetic leader says, "No terrorist group has succeeded thus far in obtaining a nuclear weapon."

Well, we'll never know what he knows, but my friends, he says that he's reduced the risk of nuclear terrorism. Do you really believe that?

Many years ago, when I was a local host on KSFO radio in San Francisco, I had the honor of interviewing Samuel Cohen, the man who developed the neutron bomb. Thanks to Sam, we had one of the greatest weapons in human history: the neutron bomb. Guess who destroyed our nuclear arsenal of neutron bombs: George Bush. King George the First deactivated all of our neutron bombs. And now take a guess who still has neutron bombs. That's right, China and Russia. So he declawed our nuclear arsenal.

Now we have a leftist academic boasting that he has reduced the risk of a terrorist getting the radioactive material to produce a nuclear weapon when we know it's a complete lie. With our weakened defenses the probability that terrorists will develop a nuclear dirty bomb has gone up. And you're worried about microaggressions on campus? You're worried about homophobia instead of the annihilation of an entire civilization?

Who are the Vikings of today who can save us? Who are those who have no conscience? The ISIS people are training their children to have no conscience. They teach them to kill from the earliest stage and feel nothing. And we teach our boys to be like girls. We teach our boys that if it feels good, do it. We teach our boys to get high on marijuana and reduce their brains to mush.

I read an article online, an article with a video: "WH Censors French President Saying 'Islamist Terrorism,'" by Craig Bannister of MRCTV. According to the article, "The White House website has censored a video of French Pres. Francois Hollande saying that 'Islamist terrorism' is at the 'roots of terrorism.'"

Why would the White House do that? Why would your man, Barack Obama, censor the words "Islamist terrorism" when they were stated not by a right-wing maniac, not by a Republican, but by a socialist president of France? Why? Why would he do that? Here's what Hollande said: "We're also well aware that the roots of terrorism"—and here is what Obama censored from the ears of the American morons—Hollande said, "Islamist terrorism, is in Syria and in Iraq. We therefore have to act both in Syria and in Iraq, and this is what we're doing within the framework of the coalition."

Your traveling president took those words out of Hollande's speech. And you think you're safe living in this country? We're the protectors of the free world, and Obama refuses to say "radical Islam." He censors the French president who says the thing that we all know to be true. Look at the video yourself.

As someone observed in the comments section under the article, "I never thought I would see the day when a French leader had more balls than an American one."

Here's another comment: "Western civilization is being invaded by Stone Age barbarians, complete with their Third World violence and disease. There is not a single nation on the face of this planet that has not been invaded and conquered at some point in their history. Up until now, there was not a single instance where the invaded nation did not fight back in an attempt not to be conquered and subjected to the culture of the invaders. Sometimes this resistance to the invaders was successful. Sometimes it wasn't. The 21st century leftist, in the face of an invasion, chooses to lay down and be conquered and subject themselves to an alien culture."

There is more that was written. It's about suicide. It's about the suicide of the West. It's about the death of the middle class.

I wrote my last book, *Government Zero*, on the relationship between the Islamists and the progressives. Why were they related, I asked, when Islamists would throw half of them down a well and kill them? Why is there no outcry among so-called progressives about the threat of Islamists? The industrial-scale rape of little Yazidi girls?

I actually was perplexed by it. I started putting two and two together, and one night it came to me in its completeness. It's really simple.

The Islamists are pagans. Despite the fact that they wrap themselves in a religion, by definition they are not Muslims. We've been told that by the president and every news organization that the Islamist terrorists are not Muslims. So I accept their word for it. They're not Muslims. They are pagans, and they are wrapping themselves in a religion in order to sell their paganism, in order to conquer the West. They are using religion as a weapon. That's their Trojan horse. Because you're afraid to say a word about their religion.

Yet we're told that they're not religious. We're told every day that they have no religion. They are pagans by definition because they are not practicing the religion of peace, are they? So if they have no religion, why are you afraid to comment on them?

What do they have in common with the Left or progressives?

Paganism.

If you look at the media leftists, they're all pagans. They practice paganism. They have eschewed the religion of their birth, if they ever had one, to worship at the golden calf of hedonism, greed, and exhibitionism. Therefore they're pagans. And therefore the pagans of the media, the pagans of the government-media complex, have a lot in common with the pagans of barbarism, in that they are all pagans who are worshipping false idols.

That's why they hate the authentic religion of Christianity in particular.

5

OUR IMMEDIATE CHALLENGES

LOW-INFORMATION VOTERS ON THE LEFT— AND RIGHT

We've heard the phrase a hundred times, that there are "low-information voters" on the left. Let me tell you something. There are an awful lot of those people on the right as well. They are as mindless and blinded as the Left regarding what people say and what they think people should say.

Unfortunately, there are now millions of low-information voters. They are defined as people who vote but who are poorly informed about politics. Many conservatives believe that "low-information voter" applies only to liberals. They're wrong.

The term was actually coined by the pollster and political scientist Samuel L. Popkin. He used the phrase "low-information signaling" in his book *The Reasoning Voter: Communication and Persuasion in Presidential Campaigns*. Low-information signaling refers to cues that affect voters' behavior in lieu of their relying on substantive information. An example would be voting for Bill Clinton because he ate at McDonald's or perceiving John Kerry and Barack Obama as elitist for going wind surfing and golfing, respectively.

Back in the 1990s, the linguist George Lakoff wrote that "low-information voter" was a pejorative term used mainly by liberals to refer to people who vote conservative against their own interests. The term assumes that voters do so because they lack sufficient information. So if you think the term "low-information voter" applies only to liberals, you're mistaken. The term was originally coined by liberals to denigrate conservatives.

The absence of information is a dangerous thing in any society, but especially in a democratic republic. But it occurs as much on the right as it does on the left. We know it applies to knee-jerk liberals. That's a given. That's how Obama got elected twice, despite standing for so many things that are antithetical to America, American values, and even America's survival. The people who love him despite all that, the people who bought into the quick, perfect smile and false, folksy speech pattern, are low-information voters.

AMERICAN VALUES ARE UNDER ATTACK

What's happening to America?

As I said before, what we're living through right now is part of the disease of the cultural revolution that started a little over a half-century ago, the spawn of radicals like Allen Ginsberg, Timothy Leary, and their ilk. They were all such silk-smooth salesmen. One pushed rampant sex with animals; another one pushed rampant drug use, mainly of LSD; the other one, God knows what she pushed.

There was also a lawyer involved. William Kunstler. Kunstler was a once respectable attorney who went on the freedom buses to the South with the hippies and had so much sex with the hippie girls that he became a crazy left-wing fanatic. He was one of the people who started the cultural revolution and led us to where we are today.

This lawyer Kunstler, who went on the *freedom* rides, became a convert to communism, liberalism, anything for the free stuff he was getting on the bus. Patchouli oil, the hippies' earthy odor of choice, is very addictive and very powerful; it has a powerful aroma, and apparently it went to his brain and overpowered his thinking.

As a result of Timothy Leary pushing drugs, Kunstler pushing a general diminution of the law and the Constitution, Bella Abzug pushing so-called women's rights, and Allen Ginsberg pushing sex with animals and children, we now have a cultural revolution that's not in its infancy anymore. It's full blown. And it's not the one that happened in China under Mao. This one is right here, right now.

So where are we with this cultural revolution? How far have we come and how far will we go on this road? Obama didn't start it, but he was put into place by the radical Left to push the revolution as far as he could.

Look around you. Listen to the war cries from the left. Watch as the cultural revolution swallows us whole. Watch violent black revolutionaries as they mask their hatred for whites in their "protests" against police. See beyond the sympathetic headlines for the "black lives matter" violent revolutionaries. Recognize that if they should further weaken our thin blue lines across America, we will see the total destruction of our society. Ruled not by the left-wing Obama and his cabal but by outright genocidal maniacs. The police are our sheepdogs, standing between us and the crazed howling wolves.

What happened to America? It looked. It listened. It watched. And it did nothing.

COMMUNISTS USE SEXUAL LIBERATION AND REPRESSION TO UNDERMINE US

The left-wing revolution has destroyed the fabric of American society.

When the new communist revolution started, people who were sexually promiscuous felt it was necessary to "do it in the road," as the Beatles sang. They still do, and the pornography has spread to mainstream "entertainment," to family relations, and even to "scientific" research. In the space of just a few years, we went from a traditional Disney fairy tale called *Frozen* to a sequel in which one of the stars supports the heroine having a same-sex love interest. How many young girls will *that* put on the psychiatrist's couch in a dozen or so years?

A lot of this came from the sexual liberation movement of the 1960s. You don't have to be a genius to figure out how that grew from the rigidity of the church, the rigidity of Christians, the rigidity of marriage, institutions, and traditions that kept people from enjoying themselves. Conservatives were seen as the cops guarding the borders between hedonism and repression. The same is true today. Anyone who is seen as a conservative now by Hollywood and the media is considered someone who will repress your sexual freedom.

Let's put it all into a sexual context, because this all began with the sexual revolution. We were warned that the way the communists would break down the walls of our society would be through the sexual revolution. Marxist social equality meant an end to gender domination, which meant that women could do everything men did. Now move forward forty or fifty years, and look where the sexual revolution has led. Is it not time to think about this so-called revolution more carefully? Not all things should revolve around your hedonistic impulses. Sometimes controlling yourself is more important than expressing yourself in certain areas. By controlling yourself, you might just affect yourself and society for the better.

Is it possible that unlimited freedom is suicide, just as unlimited repression is suicide? Like the Soviet system—wasn't that unlimited repression? We're all against unlimited repression like in Stalin's Soviet Union. Well, the opposite of that is America today, with unlimited sexual freedom. Both of them are equally damaging to the social order, and we need to strike a balance. I'm not saying let's go back to the 1950s or something like that, but let's understand that there are facts related to behavior in a society.

For instance, there's a new finding from the Centers for Disease Control and Prevention, which instead of protecting us from diseases is publishing rubbish such as this on American sex lives: women are more likely to have same-sex experiences than men. That is what the CDC is interested in. Sex with the opposite sex is clearly the dominant choice in our society, but that's not the story they tell. I'm not sure that the CDC even understands its own narrative when its minions write that many identifying as homosexual also have had *opposite-sex sex,* whatever that means.

Back to the research. Ask yourself why, in interviews with roughly 10,000 people between the ages of eighteen and forty-four, the numbers show a great increase in women's sexual experiences with other women. Is that the mark of a healthier society, do you think? Is that the direction of a society that is going to thrive? I don't think so. Dare I say that I pretty much know that it's not? Dare I say that the plunging birthrate would indicate that I am correct?

Some of that is the result of the Marxist doctrine of gender equality, that everyone should have a career, that no one should stay home and raise kids. But there's something else at work. The CDC tells us that women today are almost three times as likely to report same-sex intimacy as men. Interesting. Why is that happening in our society today? What does it have to do with the breakdown of our borders, language, and culture? How did we reach a point where the CDC is studying a thing like this? Instead of warning us about and preventing the new disease outbreaks being caused by uncontrolled immigration? This is an example of the meltdown of our science as well, the meltdown of medicine in the United States. I want the reader to learn where this is all coming from and try to stop where it is leading us.

Because when anything goes, everything goes.

RELIGION AS A TROJAN HORSE

How can Western civilization go on when our enemies are using religion as a Trojan horse to take us over? Yes, we have a belief in freedom of religion, but that's only when the word "religion" has a standardized meaning. When you say "religion," you generally think of people who believe in God and believe in doing good and believe in letting people live their lives in peace.

You say, of course, that you believe in people's freedom to express their beliefs in any way they want, Buddhist, Christian, Hindu, Jewish, and so on. Freedom of religion sounds good, but what if there's a religion that comes along that believes in order for its members to practice their freedom of religion, they have to kill you or convert you?

Well, you have to curtail that. Then you have to understand that there's no such thing as an absolute when it comes to freedom of religion. There has to be a limitation of what you mean by religion. If a religion preaches goodness, we all agree it's good. If a religion preaches death to others, then you have to say that it's not a religion but a political doctrine. This is the problem of the century.

We have a president and a media and a government that refuse to even understand the question and that certainly don't know the answer. It's up to us to educate them, is it not? Sure, we believe in freedom of religion insofar as a religion teaches peace and love and the brotherhood of man. When someone uses the concept of religion to dominate other religions through force and coercion or to take over a nation, then you have to say, "My friend, that's not a religion."

I don't care how many lawyers with twisted brains from New York University come at us, we're not going to let them get away with it. We should investigate every cockeyed lunatic from the ACLU for subversion before we let him or her take over our country any further. That's the kind of leadership we're all waiting for—someone who can actually discern reality; someone who actually knows reality; someone who's willing to stand up for reality. Can you name one politician who's willing to say what I am telling you? No, you can't, which is why you have such wonderful faith in politicians, because you can't get an iota of truth out of most of them. They're scared to death that if they say one wrong thing, they'll be out of office.

I don't even blame them. With the jackals in the media, they're afraid to say a word. But I will tell you this: we should be way past worrying about the degenerates in the media. Every man must speak his mind, whether he be a politician, a talk show host, or an unknown citizen. In order for America to be saved, there's only one thing that can save us, and that is the truth itself. I think in order to get to that truth, all of us must speak out.

IT'S NOT XENOPHOBIC TO FEAR FUNDAMENTALIST MUSLIMS

Your president, Barry Hussein Obama, has brought in more Muslim-nation immigrants than the entire population of Washington, D.C.: 680,000 of them. The gates to the United States are being thrown wide open to those who would come to dominate us. Their holy book teaches them not to love thy neighbor but to convert thy neighbor and impose the medieval system of oppression known as sharia law.

I grew up in a melting pot. I grew up in New York City. I'm an immigrant's son. We were a minority family, so naturally I grew up around minorities. When I went around Chinatown, all the signs were in Chinese, and no one feared the Chinese. No one worried that a Chinese person was going to strap himself into a suicide vest and blow up a restaurant. We figured they had their own world, their own ways, and everyone got along.

Likewise, I would go to a German bar on the Upper East Side. It was after World War II and there were memories of Hitler, but no one really thought a German would put a suicide vest on and blow up a church or an airplane. No one gave it a thought. So they spoke in German, and they had a little tendency in a direction that was a little crazy, but no one feared going to Germantown.

I can go down the list. Pick the ethnicity, pick the race, pick the religion. Nobody feared those differences in the melting pot where I grew up.

Fast forward to now, and there is one religion that the world fears: Islam. It is true that most Muslims are not terrorists. We know that. But I have to ask, why is it that every time they blow themselves up they scream, "Allahu Akbar," which is a religious statement? Why is it that they kill in the name of their religion, those who do?

Let's say that the terrorists are a small minority of fanatics. Why do they always quote their holy book, the Quran, when they do the most heinous acts you could ever imagine? Raping, murdering, kidnapping, cutting people's heads off, crucifying them in public squares, putting them into a cage, setting them on fire are all in the name of religion!

So you say to yourself, it's really not that they're different, which is what Obama would imply, or that we're xenophobic. We're not afraid of them because they're different. As I said, we're not afraid of the Chinese, we're not afraid of the Japanese, we're not afraid of the Romanians, we're not afraid of Pomeranians, we're not afraid of the Irish, English, German, or Africans.

But most people are afraid of Muslims, especially those coming into our country who make their wives wear full burkas. That's an indicator of something, isn't it? Wouldn't you say that if you were going to bring in Muslims, you would seek out the educated Muslim who has something to offer the society, someone who *wouldn't* put his wife into a fifteenth-century confining tent and treat her worse than you would treat a pet? Why would you want to degenerate a society in that direction? Why would you do that? Either you're not thinking or you actually want to set the society backward.

That is why people fear the insanity of the Democrats, who want to move immigrants from Muslim nations into this country in astonishing numbers. It is the same in Germany. No matter what happens—bombs go off, Paris gets shot up, Mali gets shot up—that psychotic Angela Merkel is still going to bring a million Muslims into a nation that is shouting "No more immigrants!"

Obama knows that this will lead to our transformation. His own State Department, which was run into the ground by Hillary Clinton, has admitted it. In early 2015, a State Department spokesperson admitted that a lack of job opportunity is a significant factor in radicalization and creating terrorists. So what has this administration done? Have you seen the employment agencies it has created for Muslim immigrants, so that when they come here they have something to do other than sit around and think about how much they hate us?

Of course you haven't. They don't exist. So why does President Hussein keep bringing them in, when even his own State Department says that bringing in unemployed Muslims creates terrorists on our soil? Where does this insanity come from? How is it that the people are ruled by such stupid, evil leaders that would go against not only the will of the people but common sense itself? Why? How? Why do such leaders exist?

I can give you a couple of answers, but all of them are so obvious that they aren't worth stating. It's not that Muslims are different. Liberals claim that anyone who fears Muslims who make their wives march around in burkas, for example, is a xenophobe. No, we're not xenophobic. We don't fear them because they're different. We fear them because we know that people who do that to their wives are likely to be religious fanatics associated with terrorism. That's what most of us feel. We're not all stupid. We all have survival instincts. And we know when we're being had and when we're being led astray. We also know when we're being put at risk. That's how we've survived this long.

THE WAR OVER GOD, GUNS, GAYS, MEXICANS, MUSLIMS, AND METROS

We are an obsessive-compulsive nation. Every topic takes forever to be resolved. Except the ones that are most damaging to us, such as the previously mentioned same-sex love in the sequel to *Frozen*.

Elections? I never saw anything like this last one; it's a joke. The whole thing, just bread and circuses, much ado about very little. What do people really care about right now? Jobs? Homeland security? No. They just want stupid jokes, pornography, titillation, stupidity. Years ago Obama said that all conservatives care about is God and guns. Well, that self-same tyrant has destroyed the concept of God completely. Put an *X* through God, and all the conservatives have left is guns. Before he leaves us, he'll try hard to take those, too, through one of his lawless executive orders. Just see the attack on our right to bear arms that Governor-Emperor Jerry Brown of Mexifornia enacted late one Friday night before running away on an extended European vacation. Like thieves in the night, these left-wing politicians take away our rights one at a time.

Yet now the paradigm has changed. Today, conservatives still care about God and guns, but they also care about gays, Mexicans, Muslims, and metrosexuals, men who are halfway to womanhood. Though not in the same way, of course. In the same way that liberals fear God and guns, conservatives fear the free pass being given everyone else.

Who can blame them? For decades, conservatives knew what they were and what they stood for. They were defined by their faith, by their family. They revered the Second Amendment, which protected those families from an oppressive government and criminals, and there was never a question that marriage was between a man and a woman. Everyone knew that. Borders were pretty ironclad. There was only one way in, and it was legal. Those were bedrock principles for what made America great. The same ideas do not operate anymore. Nobody then would have recognized conservatives of today.

See, along came the Tea Party. The Tea Party elected some people to Congress. Those representatives either did nothing or were crushed by the Left. If a man standing six foot five with a beard who looks like Paul Bunyan in a lumberjack outfit says, "Hey, I feel like a woman inside, so I'm going to the women's room," well, that's his right in San Francisco, and of course now in the rest of the United States, too. Of course, if you say anything about this, you're a bigot. In New York City, under the communist mayor, if you use the wrong honorific to address someone—if you say "Ms." and that day they feel like a "Mr."— you are acting outside the law. This is the insanity right now. This is what's happened. The world is upside down. But it didn't start with Barack Obama. It started with George W. Bush.

Dubya said he was a compassionate conservative, which was my phrase, as you well know. It wasn't good enough that there was a thing called conservatism, but he became a compassionate one. Out of misguided "compassion," we all sat back as the Left waged a relentless war on our churches, the Bill of Rights, and our traditional institutions such as marriage. We trusted our leaders in Congress to stand up to the Left, to do what we wanted them to do. We were the silent majority. Problem was, we had no representation. Our leaders didn't do what we wanted them to do. Their inactivity allowed the Left to win the culture wars.

Now here we are on the verge of literally losing our nation, erasing our borders, accepting as legal residents whole populations of individuals who hate our way of life, hate our religion, and would do us harm. We're supposed to toss our faith in God and our trust in guns to the roadside.

Remember the 1960s slogan "Better Red than dead"? The sick notion that it was better to surrender to the communists than face nuclear annihilation? Well, today, while conservatives care about God and guns and are standing firm against the fascisms of today, they are the lone bastion against the rest of the weak-kneed nation, which has embraced a philosophy of "Better Ahmed than dead." Or if you listen to Vicente Fox, the former el presidente of Mexico, we should also be chanting "Better *¿Cómo se llama usted?* than safe in our bed." Yeah, ask his name when an illegal immigrant kills you as one did Kate Steinle on the streets of San Francisco. You think that's not going to happen? Then just ignore what I'm telling you and wait. That's all you have to do—nothing—and we will be destroyed from within.

I know we're not supposed to say that. We're supposed to shy away from the obvious. After all, racists can be only of a certain race, according to everyone else on the planet. That's called cultural suicide or genocide. It's a self-genocide going on in the West. People in the West have been bullied by the radical communities into not having any pride in themselves, and now they're being stepped on by everyone else in the world.

So talk against threats is being neutralized by overreaching "hate" legislation. Meanwhile, the qualities we turn to in order to fight back—faith and firearms—are being suppressed, shamed out of our young. We're not allowed to talk about God. Obama put the toast on that one. All we cling to now are our guns, but that's not enough.

If you don't like Trump and if you don't like those of us on the conservative side, I suggest you look on both sides of the aisle and then go into the bathroom and look in the mirror. You may find an answer that you don't want to see, which is that you yourself are probably that which you hate.

The bigger point is that there are more aggressive and hateful supremacists on the other side of the aisle, there are rabid nationalists on the other side of the border, and they have nothing but contempt for the European Americans who built America.

Vicente Fox threatened war with America—and Bernie Sanders signed on for that. The idiot communist from New York, who is sort of a Stockholm-syndrome American and an honorary Latino and Mexican, said, "We cannot have a president who has insulted Latinos and Mexicans, who has insulted Muslims, who every day is insulting women in one way or another. The American people understand that bringing us together always trumps the fighting us."

The seltzer man cometh. He was very uniting, stirring up the Hispanics, the Muslims, and women—very uniting in his speech. Terrific guy. One thing about communists is that they're consistent, I will give them that.

So guard your guns and reclaim your God. When the revolution comes, we will need both.

POLITICAL DEVIANTS HAVE POISONED OUR FINEST INSTITUTIONS

More and more of what was formerly great about America is being tainted every day. When I watch movies from the 1950s, I see an America that was bold, daring, macho, unafraid, and proud of itself. But when I look at America today, I see, obviously, something else. A very small band of radical fanatical leftists has seized every aspect of the media and every avenue of government imaginable. This band is not the majority, and it doesn't speak for the people. It is a small band of deviants—deviants in a statistical sense, in a political sense, in a social sense. And these deviants in government and in the media have wrecked the United States of America and turned us into a nation of mental slaves.

How many of you dare to speak what you feel, even in your own home, anymore? You certainly can't speak what you believe at work. You would be fired because of the small band of deviants who run your workplace in the Human Resources Department. They know just where to go to listen, to spy. They know which departments to occupy to watch, to eavesdrop.

They've occupied the universities on their long march. Unlike the communist Chinese Long March of the 1930s, which covered territory, this long march is intellectual. Its course through American culture began first in the universities, because they were the softest targets. And look what they've turned them into. They're not universities with ideals anymore—not at all. These deviants have turned universities into indoctrination centers, places where deviancy is encouraged, all sorts of insanity are supported, and issues of liberty and Americanism are denigrated. Where anti-American revolutionaries are being taught to hate God, country, police, and normal sexual behavior.

After these deviants got through with the universities, their long march made its way into the government at every level, including the top position in the White House. They finally found their man, Barry Obama, and they put him into the White House. The media had long been taken over—it had surrendered without a fight, actually—so there was no opposition to be found. The media couches everything the American dictator does in ways designed to disguise his deviancy.

This small band of deviants is running America and has induced a sense of doom and fear in most of us.

Can Donald Trump's ideas reverse this? I think so. This is why the Left is so fanatically against him. They so fear a real American man who has stood up, a real American macho man, like the heroes of our films half a century ago. No one has used the word "macho." We've heard that he's an alpha male, which is a soft way of saying it, but that's not quite right. He's not an alpha male, he's a *macho* male. That's why he appeals to minority men in particular, and minority women as well, who are tired of the metrosexuals, the double-talkers, the guys with manicures—the too-good manicures. The too-good this, the too-good that. The effeminized males.

Americans—right-thinking Americans—are sick of it. They're tired of being puppets. They want someone who is bold. That's why people are waiting for the election. They can't wait. This is going to be a very, very big deal come November, we all know that.

I don't think Hillary is a viable candidate for elected office. Too much entitlement, to the manner born. If you watch her, she behaves more like Queen Elizabeth, with the little wave and the big, insincere smile. She thinks she owns the unions. But the Service Employees International Union—one of the largest unions in America, which we can thank for putting Jerry Brown into power as governor of California, virtually wiping out the opposition party in California, and causing the one-party system that exists in California today—has admitted that 62 percent of its members are identifying with Donald Trump, though they're afraid to discuss it publicly. Considering this, I think it's going to be a landslide for Trump unless the liberals rig the election completely.

But here's another problem: we can't know whether the Republican Party wants the Trump landslide to happen. I think that the boll weevils inside the Republican Party are doing what they can to help Hillary win. Why? Because a Trump victory would mean the beginning of the end of political deviancy, the end of do-nothing party politics as we know it.

America needs that.

When you have a man as statistically politically deviant as Obama (statistically in the sense that he doesn't even represent mainstream liberalism but is far to the left of it), the center slips away. It moves closer to the far, far, far left. It moves closer and closer to communism.

Then you will have a true American Long March, the kind that will lead to the same spiritual and moral darkness that has covered China for generations.

6

OUR VIRTUES

WHY I AM NOT A SOCIALIST

By all rights, I should be a socialist because I'm the son of an immigrant. I came from a poor family, and, by rights, the poor desire to take—not earn—what the rich have. But I'm not a socialist because I am also a thinking human being.

When I was a child, we were poor. I had a lot of impediments thrown at me as I grew into adulthood. I was a social worker on the Upper West Side of Manhattan, and then I was a schoolteacher. Those professions were filled with left-wing fanatics. Today, many of the people I worked with when I was younger are running New York City, or the world, into the ground. They learned nothing from history. They are stuck in amber. They fell into resin in 1969 and never came out of it. Their thinking became fossilized.

Why am I not a socialist? As the son of an immigrant who grew up in a cauldron of an immigrant community in New York that was largely left wing, you would think that I would have been a Bernie Sanders supporter. As I mentioned, I was a schoolteacher. I was a social worker. Those are jobs typically held by far-left individuals. So why am I not a socialist? Why did I become who I am, and when did it happen? I became disenchanted because I became ambitious and wanted to make something of myself. And once I expressed that desire, every impediment you could imagine was thrown into my way.

First, I was blocked from realizing my goal of becoming a college professor because of my race and sex. I was not a minority and I was not a woman and I was not a first-generation immigrant. Otherwise I might have become a very happy college teacher. Like the rest of the leeches called college teachers, 90 percent or more of whom do absolutely nothing but collect a fat check and moan and groan about how bad American capitalism is, I would have been a willing pawn in what has essentially become a gigantic brainwashing academy that destroys our youths with hatred and lies. I probably would have been one of them, happily hanging around. I'd be retired by now, and I'd have all of my friends marching around talking about how evil America is, how horrible and illiterate Donald Trump is, how brilliant Hillary Clinton is, and how wonderful Bernie Sanders is. How wonderful the "heroes" are who march, attack, and kill police.

I am not a socialist because I changed a long time ago. Unlike most of my cohorts, I evolved. They stayed in New York, and they also stayed in the ghettos of their own minds, trapped in them with the rhetoric of the 1960s, which goes back to the 1930s, which goes back to the 1880s. For them, there's nothing new under the sun. They've seen it all, they've heard it all, they're all cynical, they know everything. The irony here is that you see a billionaire like Larry David, who made $1 billion or more on the *Seinfeld* series, yet he espouses socialism. He masks himself as a socialist, as many of those from that milieu do. But let me tell you a little story about Larry David. A friend shared a small office building with him during the *Seinfeld* years. Technically, the bathroom belonged to the *Seinfeld* offices. My friend, who worked for another show, was told he couldn't use it. He had to go to another building.

See, socialism works for these guys only in the third person, not in the first person. They don't want to personally have to share.

Hollywood is filled with hypocrite activists. They all pretend they're fanatical left-wing guys while they're worth billions of dollars. How does that work? How does it work that they want more taxes and more restrictions? Because they're liars through and through. As I pointed out in the little bathroom story, they're safe in their little enclaves. They are polishing their image to sell more shows, to win more Emmys, to outshine their rivals. It's all posturing.

I evolved. I transcended that when I decided I wanted to be a success. I saw the impediments that were being put into my way by the social engineers on the left, and that's when the light started to dawn for me. That's when I realized how deadly socialism is.

The ACLU, the American Civil Liberties Union, is the worst organization in the history of the United States. It is filled with subversives, and it has done more harm to this country than all the drug cartels put together. It should be investigated by the next Republican government, brought before a grand jury, and tried for the crimes it has committed and is committing.

I'll never forget the statement from the ACLU when I was a new PhD and I applied to be a college professor. The ACLU said, "Some people have to put their careers on hold so others may advance." So they put people with lower standing, lower credentials ahead of those who, like me, had proven themselves and earned their higher standing. They intentionally skipped over better-qualified individuals and instead gave academia the underqualified generation of college professors that brought you to the debased university system we have today.

That's why, in our schools today, we don't have the blind leading the blind. We have subversives making a new generation of subversives. Men and women and transgenders whose eyes and ears and mouths are filled with hate for people who respect borders, language, and culture.

Those are the people I had to step aside for. And I thank God I did. That's what drove me into my immense success as an author and broadcaster. In any single radio show I reach and influence more people than I would have in twenty years of teaching! Unintended consequences work both ways. In trying to silence me and all the other highly qualified white males, the ACLU created a voice opposing them that is now heard around the world.

WHY CHRISTIANS AND JEWS MUST RETAIN THEIR TRADITIONS

Throughout history, societies have come and gone. Greece, Rome, the Mongols, the Third Reich—their names are legion. We're no different. The American Century is done with, over. As today's society melts down under the despot currently in the White House, people are opting out. They see the handwriting on the wall. They know that Obama is, in his own mind, a kind of Caesar, or if not a Caesar, then some kind of ruler without any opposition.

This is not the first society to live through a successive pack of liars such as Clinton, Bush, and Obama and to go up and down, because societies come and go. But through it all, ancient traditions live on. That's the important thing to understand. Why do you think Catholics cling to their rituals? Because ancient traditions give meaning to their lives and to the lives of their families and children. They don't need the entertainment industry to tell them how to live. They can take what comes from the sewer pipe of Hollywood and simply ignore it. The early Christians did that when they met in caves, secure from the eyes of Rome and the pollution of a degenerating society.

Jews, similarly, value their traditions. Consider the meaning of Hanukkah and why it matters today. According to the Hanukkah story, after the ancient Syrians ransacked the holy temple, they were thrown out by the Maccabees, who were the warrior princes of their time. The Jews came back. They kicked out the ransackers. And as they were fixing up the old temple that had been ransacked, they found a small jug of holy oil for the menorah, or lamp, at the bottom of the rubble and lit it. The holy oil was supposed to burn for only one night, but miraculously, the story goes, it burned for eight nights, which is why Jews light candles for eight nights in a row.

This year, 2016, the presidential election year, the first night of Hanukkah falls on December 24, Christmas Eve. If ever there were divine synchronicity, this is it. So what does this mean to you, running as you do so busily every day, trying to provide for yourself and your family? What this signifies for us as human beings is that no matter how distraught we may feel, no matter how wrecked we may believe our society is, there is always a small amount of holy oil left within all of us that can be reignited and carry us through the darkest hours.

That's a very important modern interpretation of Hanuk-kah, the Festival of Lights, and I thought I would share it with you because most of the ancient traditions have lost virtually all meaning for most people.

We don't live in the Age of Reason. We don't live in the Age of Enlightenment. I declare our age to be the Age of Cynicism. That is how a totally incompetent individual such as Obama can rise to the highest office in the world—because we live in an age of cynicism.

If your life is broken right now, everything is wrong, you're broke, someone in your family just died, your wife left you, you've been fired, someone important to you has been diagnosed with a disease, you don't know if you can go on tomorrow, what you've got to do is learn to reach inside yourself for that holy oil that God gave all of us when we were created. You're going to find that you have a greater inner strength, a greater inner fire, a greater ability to go on than you thought, if only you would stop, not listen to anybody else, and look within yourself. That's the meaning of the Festival of Lights. That's the meaning of Hanukkah.

WHAT IS A TWENTY-FIRST-CENTURY CONSERVATIVE?

One of the most important questions we have to ask and answer is "What is a conservative?" A lot of people think they know the answer, but they don't.

For starters, we need to stop talking about the beloved warhorses such as Edmund Burke and William F. Buckley, Jr. The old English statesman and the recent TV provocateur are dead and buried. They were conservatives *in their time*. The world has changed. The definition of what a conservative is has changed. With the emergence of ISIS, we have to redefine our terms to include challenges they never dreamed of.

Liberals do not seem to understand that they cannot be as liberal as they once were, given the threat from the Islamofascist savages. The Left has gone even more to the left, almost to the point of suffering from Stockholm syndrome. Conservatives have to decide how they're going to adapt as well. Political movements, like species, must adapt or die.

There are those who think they know what conservatism is and will tolerate only those who accept their definition. These so-called pundits believe they can apply a simple litmus test to determine who is allowed to call themselves conservative and who isn't. Anyone who doesn't subscribe to each and every item on their list—ban abortions, promote the Christian religion and values, build the military, shrink taxes—fails the test. "So-and-so is not a true conservative!" they whine in squeaky nasal voices.

I have my own definition. When I began on radio in 1994, I was asked to define what I stood for. People asked, "What do you mean by conservative?" They didn't really understand it that well. I didn't have to quote Buckley or Burke. Unlike some people, I didn't need to go to a textbook to tell anyone what I believed in. I am thinking constantly. I listen to people who call *The Savage Nation*, talk to people in restaurants and on the street. I write books.

It will come as no surprise to any of you that I define conservatism as borders, language, and culture. Tens of millions of libertarians agree with me. They say they believe in these three principles but they just don't want anyone telling them how to live. I do not know a better definition today of what conservatism is than mine.

Just as left-wing pedantic academics, "putzfessors" such as Barry Obama, are running the country into the ground while they hold offices in the executive branch, right-wing pedantic academics are sapping our ability to fight back. Ironically, I understand the historical conservatives like Burke and Buckley better than they do. Like all academics, they can squeak out isolated historical details in their thin little voices, but they miss the forest for the trees. The conservative forest has always been borders, language, and culture.

Edmund Burke did not face the same challenges we do today. Burke was a legislator in the British Parliament in the eighteenth century, when the British Empire was expanding. He supported the empire but was critical of the king or his ministers whenever they destroyed local cultures and customs. He understood, as I do today, that the essence of conservatism is borders, language, and culture.

That's why Burke opposed the East India Tea Company's actions during the First Anglo-Maratha War. The British had facilitated the destruction of not only the infrastructure of an entire region of India but of long-standing customs that were essential to the social and economic stability of the region as well. Burke understood that destroying the local pillars of civilization as it existed in India at the time would not benefit the British Empire. Did avowed conservatives such as George W. Bush and Dick Cheney understand that when they dismantled Iraq and left the pieces to be consumed by the ISIS dogs?

Burke's support of the American Revolution was based on the same principles. He supported the empire's rule over the American colonies. But he opposed the same thing the American colonists opposed in 1775: Parliament destroying long-standing legal customs by imposing new taxes and laws, when the colonies had previously reserved that authority for themselves. Eliminating those cherished legal traditions was an attack on American culture at the time, just as the progressives' attack on private property and free enterprise is an assault today.

Buckley also defended borders, language, and culture during his time, which was largely during the Cold War. The United States faced substantial threats from international communism abroad and virtually unopposed progressivism in all areas of popular culture at home. Remember, this was before conservative talk radio, when the media were uniformly liberal. The few brave conservative voices on radio and TV, men such as Joe Pyne and Alan Burke, were considered the lunatic fringe. To help defend traditional American culture, Buckley founded the *National Review*.

In the face of communist revolutions all over the world and liberal coups such as the Great Society at home, Buckley defended America's borders, language, and culture by promoting a more libertarian, laissez-faire economy at home and energetic support for anticommunist movements abroad. Those were the means to protect America's borders, language, and culture in his day.

Buckley was in his midseventies on September 11, 2001, and he died in 2008. He lived long enough to realize that the Iraq War was a tragic mistake, as I did at the time. But he didn't live to see what it and Hillary Clinton's support of the Arab Spring produced: ISIS and the all-out invasion of the West by Muslim refugees and terrorists. And just as the means of defending America's borders, language, and culture were different for Buckley during the Cold War than they were for Burke during America's colonial period, our means must be different in defending them against the Progressive-Islamist takeover we face today.

Conservatives, take note: expand your inclusiveness by shrinking your definitions. Let Donald Trump or any other self-described conservative politician stand shoulder to shoulder with three simple words:

Borders. Language. Culture.

CONSERVATIVES ARE DEFINING THEMSELVES TO DEATH

I was thinking about including a chapter on immigration. Not the legal kind that my family undertook. The other kind. We all know it's a vitally important subject. But then I realized that immigration should be in every chapter and not a stand-alone chapter. Then I thought about one aspect of immigration that needs to be singled out: If we allow our borders to fall, will there be anything of conservatism left? Wrong things, wrong people get in. Look around you. It's a process that started years ago.

There are those on the so-called right wing who think they're the pope of conservatism, who say that Donald Trump's not pure enough because he's not a social conservative. This kind of attitude was the exact attitude that predominated in Russia after the communist revolution, where they all started arguing that certain people weren't pure enough communists, remember? They talked about "counterrevolutionaries."

Early in the Republican presidential nomination process this past cycle, I was told I had made the wrong choice. The pundits attacked me. "Trump's not a conservative," they said. "If Savage supports him, then *he* is not a conservative. Only

Cruz is the real thing." At the time I said that this is the kind of limited thinking that you get out of the communists, and I believe it's truer now. We've got to get rid of conservatism as an idea. It's dead. What we need is nationalism. Let me take you back to when I was first thinking about this book and talking about what should be the first chapter. My first thought was that we should start by answering the question "What is a conservative?" I figured that would lay the groundwork for everything that came after.

Then I started thinking about the Iranian antiques dealer who was thrown into jail, the one I told you about at the start of this book. He was locked up for having the wrong political ideas, not for trying to kill people. He was a victim of the same kind of thinking that conservatives are using on the rest of us. But I realized something more insidious. While we fight each other, we are wide open to deadlier attacks from the left. Imagine what would have happened during the American Civil War if Great Britain or Mexico or Spain had attacked us. Imagine if we'd had a Hillary Clinton on our side. She'd have been the great attorney-appeaser seeking reconciliation. Can you even begin to compare her to Abigail Adams, who was nearly as vested in "Independency" as her husband, our second President? For that matter, can you imagine what Bill Clinton would have been doing in Philadelphia while Hillary was back in Massachusetts? It wouldn't have been serving on the Declaration Committee, I can tell you that. There were only men in the Continental Congress.

This debate about conservatism is an idiotic sideshow. It's a useless distraction that has to stop. We are better than that. Do you understand? Let me repeat: we are better than that. We do not need these trivial debates. They have always been distractions, since the days of the Founding Fathers. People fought duels over ideology, but it rarely had anything to do with who we are, with our core identity as Americans. Uniquely, we have the ability to harness that identity and conquer the plains or split the atom or go to the moon or create goods the world desires. That is one of our greatest strengths, if not *the* greatest.

What we should do, what a President Trump should do, is investigate all these liberal groups, not just Facebook and the IRS. A Trump administration should monitor all American mosques, stop everyone who is trying to subvert our country. Would that be conservative enough for you?

We need to do something about what the Left has done to the country. It's trying to own us. That's more than ideas. I've seen it waiting for the Supreme Court. It has damaged virtually every aspect of our government. What's wrong with something like the House Un-American Activities Committee, HUAC, like they had in the 1950s? Why is that a violation of anyone's rights? In Chapter 2, I published a long list, a very important list, of all the groups, the subversive groups, that are attacking us today. Every one of them is a dangerous, nihilistic group that has been set up specifically to violate the Constitution and undermine our republic. The only way of stopping them is first to expose them.

Conservatives: Stop fighting about definitions. Save the nation! First we have to say it can happen here, here are the subversive groups, here is what we must do. First, unmask them.

Then hold committee hearings under the new administration and investigate their money sources.

Definitions. How do they matter in the face of real danger? You want to define something? We expose the groups that subvert, that are clearly set up to subvert the will of the people. They are an active minority of radical communist Marxists, who usurp the entire meaning of democracy. They've literally railroaded their agenda down our throats. We have to unmask them, so we've been doing that by naming them. We've called out the subversive groups, we've named them. We're shaming them. Call it "name 'em and shame 'em." We're going to show, in a short couple of paragraphs, what each has done. We're going to demand that there be a congressional investigation of all those subversive groups with regard to their funding. We're going to find out how many of them have received federal funds, how many have received private funds from illegitimate sources.

Notice that I didn't say we should throw them in jail. I said let's expose them and expose their funding. That's as far as I'll go. If jail is merited, if the government's going to investigate that possibility at all, it first has to find evidence of a crime. And guess what: if those groups are getting funding by breaking campaign finance laws and other financial laws, we're clearly there. If they have committed other crimes, we'll find that out too.

Conservatives: Dismantle the circular firing squad. Turn your fire outward so we can start to restore what is dearest in American society.

THE REAL CONSTITUTION

When I talk about borders, language, and culture being the bedrock of conservative thought, you may say I'm omitting things such as the Constitution. You know, the document that was apparently written by black men and not middle-aged white guys, if you believe the Broadway rap musical *Hamilton*. I don't have to bang the Constitution over your head like a Bible, do I? The idea behind borders, language, and culture automatically references the Constitution. That definition of conservatism contains everything conservatives are trying to *conserve*. It is our borders, language, and culture that define who we are: they are the product of long traditions such as private property, individual liberty, and the rule of law. The Constitution is the result of our borders, language, and culture, not the other way around.

The United States has a written constitution that defines what the government is supposed to do and how it is supposed to do it. And what limits those in power. But the smug academics who use it as a bludgeon don't seem to understand why the Founding Fathers wanted a written constitution in the first place: to prevent the government from destroying America's borders, language, and culture the way so many tyrannical governments had in the past. The Constitution—a document that the constitutional "scholar" Barack Hussein Obama has fought hard to suppress—strictly defined what the government would do and forbade it to do anything else. Which is why Obama has worked around it and through it, shredding it along the way.

The Founding Fathers—I refuse to use the currently fashionable word "Founders," which I guess is meant to be inclusive of women and slaves—the Founding *Fathers* wrote it the way they did for one reason, one incontrovertible reason: because they were conservatives.

7

OUR SHAME

WATCHING SAILORS APOLOGIZE
FOR BEING CAPTURED

"It was a mistake. That was our fault, and we apologize for our mistake."

"Your GPS said that you had penetrated to Iran territorial water?"

"I believe so."

"How was the Iranian behavior with you?"

"The Iranian behavior was fantastic while we were here. We thank you very much for your hospitality and your assistance."

That was the most humiliating moment in my lifetime as an outsider, as a civilian, watching the US Navy sailors seized in January 2016. I had never seen anything like it in my entire life, and even today we don't yet have the full, humiliating, possibly criminal story. It reminded me of the propaganda films from the Korean War, when the communists would capture soldiers and torture them. The same, smooth off-camera voice saying "You are well treated by us. You have no problem?" Secretary of State John Kerry gets up and thanks them in his double-talking way, wearing his suit of ketchup, with his silk tongue and his silk mouth and his silk brain, and no one in the media says anything.

No one's asking these questions: Did they go aground because an EMP weapon disabled the naval boats? Did they go aground because they were off course? How could a naval boat go off course when it's manned by sailors who are so skilled at driving those things? I, as a small-craft boater, have gone aground just once because I had no chart going into a harbor. It can happen to a civilian, but it's impossible to believe that it would happen to two US Navy boats at once. It's impossible to believe that, unless they were given the wrong charts for the area or somebody screwed with their GPS. There's no other way it could have happened.

What mother ship did those fast patrol boats come from? They don't launch out of the air. Some amphibious craft probably held those boats. Who's the captain? He is responsible for this. The boats were fast assault craft, CB90 combat boats. They were originally developed by the Swedish Navy. The CB90 is a very fast and agile boat, can turn very quickly, can decelerate from top speed to a full stop in 2.5 boat lengths. It's lightweight, with a very shallow draft, which means it can go into shallow water. It runs off a jet engine, meaning twin water jets, and can run up to speeds of 40 knots, 74 kilometers an hour, in shallow coastal waters.

So how did it happen? How did a boat of this advanced nature wind up going aground on an Iranian island in the Persian Gulf? How was that even possible? We were told that one of the boats had engine failure but not why. Were the engines tampered with? Why was a major warship and air cover not immediately sent to protect the boats and tow them away from the Iranian patrol boats?

No one's answering these questions. They need to be answered. They will never be answered by the café singer in the White House who applauded himself over and over and over again that night, creating a parallel universe the way every other dictator in history has done, talking about a paradise that doesn't exist. He went on and on and on about how wonderful the world is and how everyone who opposes him is the enemy. To the café singer, that silky lounge lizard, there are no enemies except the internal enemy.

This is the same White House that washes its hands of ISIS and says it's nothing. They won't even say the enemy is Islamic. Every time those monsters kill somebody or blow something up, they say they're doing it in the name of Allah, they say they're doing it in the name of Islam, and he says, "One of the world's religions." No, not involved at all. How's that for a big lie. *Another* big lie?

We were warned that the day would come when big lies would be repeated over and over and over again. Hitler's propaganda minister, Joseph Goebbels, said, "If you tell a big lie often enough, it will become the truth." From the smallest police chief to the biggest liar in the world, the same big lie is being told: that the chaos in the world has nothing to do with religion. It's just killers and fanatics. It's nothing to do with religion and we have nothing to fear from them.

Oh? Isn't Iran a Muslim theocracy?

My friends, it gets worse by the day, doesn't it? Photos were released by Iran state TV from the moment the US sailors were captured and bent down on their hands and knees, because they wouldn't even fire a shot to save themselves. Why did they not fight it out? Why didn't they shoot their way out of that situation? They had the guns. Why didn't they use them?

The whole thing was a setup, that's why.

During a speech in which Obama talked about ISIS in a parallel universe, I happened to be at dinner. I tried not to watch the speech. I couldn't take it. He wouldn't even mention the word "Islam." The man seems to be allied with Iran! There's no other conclusion. Either he's living in a delusional world, or he's a double agent. There's no other explanation for making a speech like that. He denied what had happened in San Bernardino, he denied what had happened in Boston, he denied what had happened to the cop in Philadelphia, he denies the number of ISIS-related events, he disconnects ISIS from Islam. Every rational, literate human being on earth says they're Islamic. Even the terrorists say it. Why can't he?

If this is not the work of a propagandist for the enemy, tell me what *would* be the work of a propagandist for the enemy. To see the men on their hands and knees apologizing to the religious dictators who run Iran, and to see Kerry thanking Iran for returning the troops that had been delivered to Iran on a silver platter, it's clear there is something very wrong with the country under this delusional sociopath in the White House.

I ask myself as I write this, will I be understood or will I be misunderstood? Can the brainwashed fools on the liberal side ever comprehend that they have been had, that their lives are being put into danger by this administration that they seem to worship so much?

Ladies and gentlemen, you are witnessing the destruction of the US military by the greatest enemy of our freedom. Two very advanced US naval craft suddenly wander into the middle of the Persian Gulf and go aground at the same time. Our good friends in Iran, the good friends of John Kerry, "rescue" our sailors, but not before stealing all of our latest technology and humiliating our people.

Let me tell you something, and remember it carefully: in my estimation, there is a double agent inside this. It is somebody inside the Obama administration who did this to the US Navy. That agent did it to us with one of our most advanced drones two years ago. You may have forgotten that already because you have no press other than a few men left in the media, a few websites left where you can find the truth. Somebody in the administration sent our most advanced drone to Iran two years ago. It landed without a scratch, like a new Buick in a showroom. Our most advanced drone was delivered on a silver platter to the Iranians on the watch of that smiling puppet on the stage, that lying smiling café singer getting away with murder and treason.

The self-congratulatory speech that Barack Obama gave after that humiliating incident was in another universe—it came from somewhere else. He was living in an alternate universe. He was talking about a world that doesn't exist, and the sycophants in the Republican Party couldn't applaud enough. I accept it from a Nancy Pelosi and the other fetid creatures from the jungle floor. I can scent their subversion through the TV screen. I accept it from the Democratic Socialists. But I couldn't believe I was watching the Republicans applauding. He walked down the aisle smiling as though he were on a red carpet in Hollywood. The world is burning around him, and this double agent tells us the world is perfect.

All I could think of was Josef Stalin when he was confronted with boys being raped and murdered on a railroad track in the 1950s. Stalin told the commander to remind his underlings, "There is no homicide in paradise. It only happens in a capitalist nation."

I was watching that during the State of the Union speech, in which the café singer delivered a speech about a paradise that doesn't exist. Barry Hussein Obama is a small replica of other power-mad dictators. A form of religious genocide by silent complicity is being committed against Christians because the maniac in the White House won't lift a finger to protect them. He's a silent accomplice to the genocide going on against Christians in the Middle East, and he doesn't even talk about it. He tells us that the Iranians are our friends. They're our great friends. Well, friends don't supply arms and IEDs to terrorists. Iran does. They are used to kill innocent Christians and US soldiers.

Did you see the Navy men humiliated? Did you see them bowing down to the Iranian murderers, the same way our president bowed to the Saudi king a few years back? Did you see them then saying how well they had been treated in a prison camp? Do you know that behavior like this in another time would have been considered sedition? They might have been court-martialed when they came back, tried and executed for catering to the enemy. And it happened on the very day that the fraud gave the big smiling speech, the big smiling Obama, glad-handing down on the runway.

I don't understand where America went. It went up in smoke, without a fight, without protest from the media. This is not a right-wing view. This is a practical view. How can anyone see and yet not understand what just happened to this military? Two boats suddenly conk out and run aground, and they're rescued by Iran. The nine men and one woman aboard were detained by the Islamic Revolutionary Guards on Farsi Island. The unnamed sailor said it was a mistake: "It was our fault, and we apologize for our mistake." I ask again, can anyone explain to me how those boats died and ran aground? They are the most advanced naval watercraft imaginable. How did they die? Anyone who is a boater knows it was sabotage. *Those boats don't conk out.*

In the second novel of my Jack Hatfield series, *A Time for War*, one scene opens with a US military helicopter suddenly plummeting to earth in Afghanistan because a Chinese device had this revolutionary technology that could stop the rotors from turning. A Chinese agent fused the helicopter components and the helicopter crashed.

A few scenes later, an FBI car is pursuing the bad guys in San Francisco. The police car stops in the street because a bad guy has a device that he presses a few keys on and it stops the computers from operating in the police car.

With our sailors? My guess is that somebody gave the codes to the Iranians, who then jammed the boats' computer systems, the computer systems stopped the boats, they went aground, they were given to the Iranians on a silver platter. Our advanced technology was given to the Iranians, just as it was with the drones. Then we see the apology, and then we hear John Kerry congratulating himself for his great relationship with the terrorists in Iran. And nobody in the media sees the bigger picture.

Obama's not a sellout; he's giving America away for free.

PUTIN PRESSES IN SYRIA WHILE OBAMA JUST BENDS

"**A**s president of the United States, I am mindful of the dangers that we face. They cross my desk every morning. I lead the strongest military that the world has ever known."

Well, Barry's almost right. There's one little piece missing: "I *mis*lead the strongest military that the world has ever known."

He has purged the military. Josef Stalin executed his generals in the 1940s out of fear that they were plotting a coup against him, which they were not, and as a result the Soviet military was unable to operate effectively. Similarly, other dictators have purged the military in paranoid fits. Hitler, for one. Kim Jong-un, the power-mad ruler of North Korea, for another.

Today we are witnessing a similar purge, carried out not with bullets but with smears, innuendo, and spurious legal charges. But it is a purge of senior military officers nevertheless. The chapter "Zero Military" in my prescient book *Government Zero* is a must read. I actually named the generals that Barry has purged in order to foster the progressive Islamist takeover of the United States of America and the world. They have names.

The administration has continued right from where my last book left off. Barry has eliminated one seasoned combat leader after another through smears and innuendos. He has demilitarized our military. It's all part of the progressive Islamic takeover of America—attacking at the core, another step in the ongoing purge and reconstruction of the military. The Obama administration continues its quest to transform the military from an institution of patriotic warriors largely inspired by Christian principles into an atheistic, multicultural, progressive bureaucracy where male marines receive sensitivity training in order to fight next to female marines.

My heart beats with sadness to see what's happened to this country and this military under this radical extremist in the White House. My personal feeling is that at the end of the day, now that Russia is so deeply enmeshed in the Syrian civil war, that country will constrain Hezbollah. I think

Russia will be a stabilizing force in the Middle East rather than a destabilizing force. The greatest destabilizing force in the Middle East has been Barry from Honolulu and Hillary from Chappaqua. He came into office with zero foreign policy experience and learned nothing on the job. Hillary did even worse: she ignored anything she learned as a New York senator and used the State Department to enrich foreign donors to her foundation.

When will you wake up to the fact that we have a sociopath in the White House who has destroyed the Middle East and wrecked our borders, language, and culture. Yet he had the nerve to say the gravest threat to the world is global warming. Not ISIS, which has conquered a territory larger than Great Britain under his watch—if you want to call it his watch. Its fighters have raped and pillaged and beheaded their way across the Middle East.

Finally Putin said, "That's enough. You're not getting Syria. You're not taking out Assad. You're not taking away our warm-water ports. Period. End of story." And he, frankly, began to do the job that Obama said he himself was doing. Hey, we still have a warm-water port, a bunch of them in Hawaii, where Barry from Honolulu bodysurfs on his endless vacations.

But again Barry was lying. He was not doing the job against ISIS. If he's been conducting air strikes for more than two years, as he and the empty suits in his administration have been saying, why is ISIS still able to strike us at home? You're telling me our Air Force is that bad? We have the greatest Air

Force in the world. At least we did until Barry took over. Do you know who's running the Air Force now? A woman who never piloted an airplane! A glorified air traffic controller, that's who! He handpicked her as he did Loretta Lynch to feminize the Air Force, along with the Navy and the Marines, but the fact of the matter is that anyone can see that even though we have been bombing Syria for years to take out ISIS, we have failed.

So who has failed? Is it the brave young kids who fly the jets? No, it's not them. They could have taken ISIS out in a week. Many of them have even said so after they quit the Air Force because they couldn't believe what they were being forced to do.

It's not the young men flying our jets who have failed in taking out ISIS. It's the commander in grief, the greatest thief of our sovereignty in the history of this republic. And I'm not saying that just to be glib. The thin man in the White House is the problem. The problem is Barry Obama from Honolulu, who is in so far over his head that even his most devout supporters recognize that the world is going up in flames.

At the United Nations something even more remarkable happened. As you know, England's former prime minister, David Cameron, and Obama are on the same page with regard to almost everything. Yet Cameron of England and Obama, who were debating Islamic extremism at the United Nations, had a little disagreement because Obama would not say one word about radical Islam. Even Cameron could not believe what he was listening to.

Barry said, "Violent extremism is not unique to any one faith, so no one should ever be profiled or targeted simply because of their faith. Yet we have to recognize that ISIL is targeting Muslim communities around the world."

Cameron answered back, "You said—and you're quite right—that every religion has its extremists. But we have to be frank that the biggest problem we have today is the Islamist extremist violence that has given birth to ISIL, to al-Shabaab, to al-Nusra, al-Qaeda, and so many other groups."

Even milquetoast Cameron—the same guy who categorically *would not meet* with Donald Trump until suddenly he would—had to step out of his loafers and say, "Even I can't swallow this one." Again, Obama won't say Muslim, Islam, and extremism in the same breath.

So we are in a new world right now. Putin has pulled the trigger. Russia began its air strikes using Su-34 Fullback bombers. The biggest fear is that there will be a clash between US fighter jets and Russian fighter jets over Syria. That would be the worst possible outcome. Russia demanded that the United States stop its own air strikes, which is a joke unto itself. Excuse me, what air strikes? Then we heard the secretary of misstatement, John Kerry, and the others trumpeting the air strikes of the last years against ISIS, while ISIS has metastasized and morphed into worldwide terrorist attacks. What air strikes? Which aspirin factories was Obama blowing up with our jets, wasting the precious resources of our fighter pilots on a charade, a paper war against ISIS? We know that he's not fighting ISIS, which is why ISIS has grown.

Many of us believe that he has actually funded ISIS, supplied weapons to ISIS, and that ISIS is Obama's army, set up specifically to take down Syrian President Assad. When I started saying this, many of you thought I was crazy. But little by little the truth of that has come to light, has it not? So the United States said to Russia, "No, we're not going to stop our air strikes. We're going to continue them." But, what exactly is the Democrats' strategy for the Middle East? Obama is bumbling, and we pray to God that the American people are smart enough not to replace him with Hillary Clinton. Never forget it was Clinton's Arab Spring that let religious rivalries flourish, starting a regional meltdown and the world's refugee crisis.

There are so many related elements to this story, including speeches by U.S. leaders as they come forward with their double-talk—Kerry; Secretary of Defense Ash Carter, who's only defending his idiot boss—and it's all about what? What's it really about? It's about bringing down Assad.

Let's face it, Assad is a dictator. He's a very, very dangerous man, but he's not going anywhere because he is a puppet of Russia, and a useful puppet of Russia at that. Telling Russia to abandon Assad would be the equivalent of telling the United States to get rid of Israeli prime minister Netanyahu. Don't get me wrong, I'm not putting Assad and Netanyahu into the same class of humanity. But do you think you're going to convince the Russians to abandon Assad? Why should they? And who is Assad? He is not a Sunni Muslim. He is a Shia, an Alawite, which is a branch of Shia Islam. He has never really been a follower of Islam. He's a scientist, a doctor. He was not educated in a madrassa, as was Obama. Did you know that Obama is probably more of a Muslim than Bashar Assad? Assad never went to a madrassa. Obama went to a madrassa in Indonesia.

Assad was educated at the Arab-French al-Hurriya School in Damascus, where he became fluent in English and French. He went on to study medicine at the University of Damascus and graduated in 1988. He conducted his residency in ophthalmology at a military hospital outside Damascus. He then attended postgraduate studies at Western Eye Hospital in London, England. His father had been grooming his brother, Bassel, as the future president, but in 1994 Bassel was killed in an auto accident and Bashar was recalled to Damascus to begin being groomed for the throne.

And you should know this: Bashar al-Assad is even more moderate than his father, Hafez, who was also a moderate monarch. By the way, history shows us that Syria is one of the more tolerant of the Levant states, along with Jordan. He's a dictator, all right, and he certainly knows how to take care of the Islamists in his country, but make no mistake about it, it was the Arab Spring, initiated by Hillary Clinton and funded by George Soros, that brought about the nightmare of what's going on in Syria.

So where does all this leave us? How did our relations with Syria get so bad? The fact of the matter is that there was a time when Syria was not on our hit list. No, not at all. What happened to change that? In 2009, US relations with

Syria turned negative. What happened in 2009? Barry from Honolulu became president. Barry from Honolulu refused to help Syria expel former Iraqi al-Qaeda fighters. Barry from Honolulu claimed that al-Qaeda was composed of innocent civilians. So before we go on and paint Assad as the evil devil, let's compare our current administration and Assad.

We're witnessing an unprecedented situation in which a foreign power, Russia, starts air strikes without notifying the United States and then tells our military to get out of the way. And our military puts a physics professor and contractor in charge of the Department of Defense. That's Ash Carter—a brilliant man in physics; Harvard University; let us say a wonderful scholar in his field; worked as an adviser to military contractors for years. In case you don't know who Ash Carter is, he used to work for old Jimmy Carter. Long time Wobbly; lifetime left-wing fanatic; game player; bumbler.

I heard him speak once. I was screaming. I said, "If I were listening to this and I were a Russian leader, I would be laughing at America." It's bad enough having these girls talk, now we have this guy, the head of the military, who comes out in a pink tie. On the day he's supposed to stand up for US military might, he comes out in another pink tie and goes on and on, saying "Well, we don't personally see it in the same way they do, and I would hope that Russia would see it in our way and come to the—" I never heard anything like that. No one speaks that way. These are bureaucrats—academic bureaucrats—who are deeply ingrained in the structure of the country. Especially the military, which has been purged by Barry.

The purge has been going on for quite a while. I told you before about how Josef Stalin executed his generals in the 1940s out of fear that they were plotting a coup against him. But they were not, and as a result of those purges, the Soviet military became unable to operate effectively. Other dictators have purged the military in paranoid fits. Today we're seeing the same thing going on with our military, a purge carried out not with bullets but with smears, innuendos, and spurious legal charges. But it is nevertheless a purge of senior military officers.

Why is Obama doing this? Why is this purge going? Because Barry from Honolulu wants to transform the military from an institution of patriotic warriors largely inspired by Christian principles into an atheistic, multicultural, progressive bureaucracy. Not only do Barry and his flunkies purge competent, battle-hardened officers and replace them with progressive academics such as Ash Carter, they also purge chaplains committed to their faith and replace them with pseudo chaplains who are willing to accept the progressive worldview regardless of their faith. They are expected to be enthusiastic about Islam even though it's the ideology inspiring the maniacs that our military is supposed to be fighting.

We turn now to what's going on in the Middle East specifically: Russian air strikes against Free Syrian Army forces, not ISIS. Oh, really? The *New York Times* put out the big smear that Russia has no intention of taking out ISIS, which is ludicrous. This is just a prelude to taking out ISIS. I'm no military expert, but I certainly have studied military issues long enough to see how the game is played. You don't go after your primary enemy when there's another force on the ground that may stand in your way or harm your own soldiers unless you're a doofus. What you do is, you take out the forces on the ground that may not be friendly to your forces and get rid of them, sweep them away, then go after your primary target.

Right now the Free Syrian Army can do grave damage to Russian troops who will be on the ground, if they're not already there. And the Russians want to have a clear field. They want to go after ISIS fighters and kill them. They will not bring them back and let them spew their Islamic hatred for the West. They're going to kill them on the field.

So do you agree with me that the enemy of our enemy is our friend? Who is our greatest enemy in the world? Is it Russia? Russia wasn't our greatest enemy until Obama messed things up and made it a personal vendetta. Russia was our ally. The Cold War was over. Things were going well. We had great trade and interaction with the Russian people and the Russian leadership. Then this bungler came along, surrounded by his dumb sorority, and now we have a Cold War turning into a hot war.

No, it's not Russia that is our greatest enemy. It's radical Islam. The Islamist ISIS. It's the greatest enemy of civilization since Adolf Hitler. So if Russia's willing to do the job, what's wrong with that? Tell me why you would oppose that.

Of course you're going to tell me what you've read in the *New York Times* and then heard ad nauseam all over the media from CNN's Barbara Starr and other bovine members of the female persuasion: "They're not taking out ISIS. They're taking out the Free Syrian Army." Well, look at the long-term strategy, Barbara, because once the Russian troops sweep the Free Syrian Army away, they'll go after ISIS. That's my guess.

Of course, we don't know what might happen tomorrow. My gravest fear is that there'll be an accidental dogfight between Russia and the United States in the Middle East or elsewhere, like when their fighters buzzed our Navy in April 2016. A shoot-down in those circumstances would be a nightmare for all of us.

The way to avoid that is for Barry Obama to actually pay attention to the papers that cross his desk every morning, instead of planning his next visit to the beach.

HOW A TOP SECRET CALLER BLEW HILLARY'S COVER

I get a wide range of callers—all ages, from all parts of the country. Some of them want to vent, a few of them want to argue; I've pretty much heard it all. But once in a while there's someone who surprises me. Someone like the man you're about to meet.

I'm going to print our conversation pretty much verbatim, because the content was as extraordinary as the caller. It began when I came off a monologue and decided to go to the phones.

"Now, let's get back to some of my callers. Bert in Utah, what you have to say is original—never heard it before. You claim you have twenty years' national top secret security clearance. I have no reason to doubt you. You connected all of this up to follow the money and the gold standard. Bert, please, for the sake of continuity, start from the beginning. You have a full five minutes right now if you need it."

"Well, the reason I'm calling you is because I'm about to make it my life's work to put Barack Obama, Eric Holder, John Kerry, Hillary Clinton in prison, and if I end up missing, I want this information out. Long story short, Nixon took us off the gold standard, changed our currency from an asset-backed currency to a commodity as a petrodollar. He approached the royal family in Saudi Arabia, he approached the Egyptians—they were the two dominant forces in the Middle East. He sold them on the idea of the petrodollar. Got all the other Arab countries to fall in line. We put the shah into Iran, we put Saddam Hussein into Iraq, we put Gaddafi in Libya, and for decades we were controlling everything. That's how the US dollar became the reserve currency and everybody that wanted to buy oil from the Middle East had to buy the US dollar to trade it for oil, so it became a commodity. Well, the Arab culture—if you take two Arabs that hate each other more than anyone else, the one group that they hate more is the infidels. So even the Arab enemies will work together to cut out the infidels. So Gaddafi and Hussein got together, and they developed what they called the gold dinar, that was to replace the petrodollar. So they wanted people to buy the gold dinar, which they would trade for oil. When they started doing this, Gaddafi got taken out, Hussein got taken out, and we started screwing around over there again. Assad is one of the few regimes over there that was duly elected. He wouldn't play ball with us. So as we do, we play both sides against each other. The CIA trained both the rebels and a false flag force that was represented as Assad's people. Hillary Clinton—"

"Wait. Hold on, Bert. That's an important point. We know that the CIA trained the so-called rebels to bring down Assad, because McCain accidentally leaked that, even though it had been leaked before. You're now alleging on this national show that the CIA set up a fake group? What's the name of that group?"

"They were represented as Assad's people."

"Okay, so they set up a fake Syrian army allegedly under the direction of Assad, and they did what? They gassed their own people?"

"If you remember, Dr. Savage, when the media reported that Assad was gassing the rebels . . ."

"Yes."

"They did an independent study on the gas. The gas that was used was not the same kind of gas that Assad had in his arsenal. It was gas that was being transported through Libya and through Turkey to these rebels because they wanted to stage an attack against the rebels that would enrage everybody. So the US shipped gas over there, had them fighting the rebels and the rebels fighting the false force and framing Assad."

"Wow. Okay, I got it. So let's bring it up to today. Is Assad as bad as ISIS? Worse? Or is he actually not as bad as we think?"

"Ask that again, please?"

"Is Assad—who is being made into the Hitler of our time

by Obama—is he as bad as ISIS or worse than ISIS? Which side should we be on, Bert?"

"He's not as bad as our government and our media's making him out to be, but he wouldn't play ball with us, and so we're framing him just like we framed all the rest. When we took out Noriega in Panama—I mean, you go through the whole history, and these are dictators and things that the US has put into place, and when they start stepping out of line, then we have to go in and remove them. And so Assad was duly elected. He won the majority vote. But then all the meddling that the US has done over there has so discredited him that the whole world's turning against him. And Russia knows better, which is why they're over there now defending him. But one of the points I want to make is when Chris Stevens found out about these weapons of mass destruction, the gas that was being smuggled in there, and the CIA's involvement, he threatened to expose it. And he was—"

"Wait, you're saying that the ambassador to Libya in Benghazi, who was beaten to death by a mob, you're saying they unleashed the mob on him because he was going to expose the United States' double dealing in all of this?"

"Yep. And Chris Stevens and his assistant—I'm in my car, I don't have my notes, Sean Smith, I think it was—were the only two in the conflict that were killed. And then the CIA outpost that was a few blocks away, they blocked any aid coming to the conflict. Chris Stevens and his aide were locked in a safe room by one of the consul employees where one of them died, one of them was unconscious from smoke inhalation. And then the two SEALs that were trying to defend the CIA outpost that were killed, they were killed because the CIA was not supposed to be taking action. They were supposed to be lying down and let Chris Stevens be taken out."

"Do you think that any of this is in Hillary's emails?"

"If they can find all the emails, they will. But, you know, Congressman Jason Chaffetz and Senator Mike Lee are neighbors of mine in Utah. When Jason was on the first committee investigating Benghazi, I told him about this. He started investigating Hillary, and he and his family were threatened to stop the investigation or they would pay for it."

"Bert, who threatened them?"

"Hillary's people."

"Mmm. Interesting. All right, so for the average listener out there—I'm following every beat of your heart—where does that leave us with regard to the average person who's watching this go on? Is Russia our natural ally in the fight against radical Islam? I think so."

"I think that's a very strong possibility."

"Okay, but we know that's not the end game of Putin. I mean, you're a man who knows the inside of all—we know Putin's an ex-KGB head, and we know that he wants to expand Russia's power. That's a given. But isn't it true also that his ally now, Iran, wants to kill ISIS because ISIS is Sunni and they're Shia? Isn't that at basic level true?"

"Well, it's like I said, Dr. Savage, another Arab is much higher than any of the infidels. Even though—you know, Putin can go in there offering all the help he wants, but he's still an infidel. So when it comes down to either Shiite or Sunni choosing another Arab over the infidels, they'll choose the other Arab."

"So you're actually stating that after the Iranians come into Syria, they're liable to join with ISIS and attack the Russians?"

"I don't know if they would go that far at this point, because Putin has built up such an incredible military while we've been diminishing ours. You know, Obama is anti-Christian, anti-Semitic, anti-Israel, anti–free market, anti-Constitution— nothing he has done is conceived for the betterment of America. While he's been deteriorating our military, Putin has been building his up at light speed. You know, there was a reason that all the BRIC countries have denounced the US dollar as reserve currency. China no longer recognizes it as reserve currency. Neither does Russia. Neither does Australia. Neither does India. Neither do most of the world powers. And so as we lose our standing as the reserve currency, there's gonna be huge economic repercussions."

"Well, look, Bert, everything you have said is not news to me with regard to Obama. I know what he wants to do. You know it, I know it. Every intelligent human being knows what he is. How does he get away with it?"

"I have no idea. I know he's a puppet. I know there are much bigger forces that are pulling his strings. I don't know if they're so deeply connected that they can defend him. But he has committed several acts of treason. I don't understand why the FBI isn't going in there with the Department of Justice and arresting him and pulling him out of the White House.

He has made a joke of the Constitution. He's made a joke of America. He's weakened our position. He's alienated all our allies. He's sucking up to the Cubans and to Iran. I mean, how blind is the American public that they cannot see that he is selling us down the river, and if we don't do an about-face damn quick—"

"Well, Bert, I can see why you're a regular listener to my program, but you're preaching not to the choir but to the preacher of the choir. I can only say you've elucidated the dollar connection. The gold standard and all that, that's something new. But the truth is, the gas thing is something new, the fake army that you say the CIA set up to make Assad look bad, I didn't know about that, although I've heard hints of that on various and sundry websites. Is there anything else that you want us to know?"

"I want the world to know that Chris Stevens was assassinated by US-trained forces and Hillary and the CIA were behind it."

"Well, I wish you luck in your hiding place, somewhere deep in the heartland of America. You must lead a very proscribed life, I would think."

"I am sick and tired of this and it may get me killed, but I am not gonna stand for it anymore."

"Wow."

"I'm gonna start exposing these people."

My conversation with Bert ended there. I would have sent him one of my books, but I didn't think he'd want to give me his specific whereabouts. He needs to protect himself so this very valuable information can get out, so his work can continue.

I will say this, though. He said he was from Utah. There is a lot of US intelligence activity in Utah. The Intelligence Community Comprehensive National Cyber-security Initiative data center is based there. So I believe he really could have known what he talked about.

I never heard from him again. I hope he's okay.

8

OUR COMPLACENCY

SURVIVAL OF THE FITTEST: WILL THE VICTORS SPEAK ARABIC?

As I've been saying, we have become a nation of global do-nothings, and I mean that in both senses of the word. We are virtually inert around the world, and we do nothing to preserve and protect our borders, language, and culture at home. Americans are hyphenate-active; that is, they will support their non-melting-pot qualities. They wave African flags, Mexican flags, gay flags. They do so with enthusiasm and selfish, narcissistic focus. To them, the American flag is something you wear on a bandanna or burn. Our complacency as Americans is leading us to doom. Do you want proof? Look across the ocean, at Europe.

There's no Great Britain anymore. We don't know yet if the Brexit vote came in time to save it or just to slow its demise. The mountains of refugees are already ashore. The social decay is in place to happen. And if Hillary wins, we're next. Can't you already hear her quoting Emma Lazarus at her inauguration, defending the flood of refugees by quoting Emma Lazarus's *The New Colossus*, quoting it with that false sincerity she has not quite mastered: "Give me your tired, your poor, Your huddled masses yearning to breathe free, The wretched refuse of your teeming shore." That was partially true when America was not a welfare magnet. Do the millions of immigrants whom Obama has flooded into our nation all work? Of course not!

The Arabs are taking over Great Britain, they're taking over the Middle East, and they're going to take over America. Yes, these are harsh words and sure to excite the ire of the thought police, but the evidence is in the headlines.

Trevor Phillips, who used to run Great Britain's Equality and Human Rights Commission, has said that he "got almost everything wrong" about the threats Muslims represent to indigenous populations. He added that adherents to Islam create "nations within nations" wherever they land. They have no interest in assimilating.

Now, some may say that this is no different from what other people have done, like the Chinese and the Hasidic Jews, creating closed communities. The big difference, of course, is that those other groups aren't encouraging homicide and conquest as a way of life.

There was a study that came out in England entitled "What British Muslims Really Think." You can look it up, but here are some interesting points: 39 percent of British Muslims think a woman should always obey her husband; 31 percent say a man should be able to have more than one wife; and nearly one-quarter believe that sharia law should be introduced into the country, as opposed to following the laws of the British Parliament. Muslims and non-Muslims disagree about marriage and relationships, school governance issues, free expression, and whether violence is appropriate when defending religion.

We could have guessed that last one. We've seen it in action enough times.

Over here, Arabic is the fastest-growing language in the United States of America. How is that possible? How is it that Arabic and Urdu, Pakistan's national language, are the fastest-growing foreign languages spoken in the United States of America? How is it even possible that Obama is allowed to do this to us? How is it possible that Barack Hussein Obama is importing more than a quarter of a million—280,000—Muslim immigrants a year? And they're bleeding us dry, even the ones who aren't fighting: 91.4 percent of recent refugees from the Middle East are on food stamps. They're deadbeats. It's another way of subverting the United States that fits neatly into the worldview of Obama. It's a view of most progressives, that borders are an inconvenience to *pax humana*.

Nonetheless, let me repeat: these people are deadbeats. I know that will shock good liberals. I realize we're not allowed to say what the facts tell us is true. But who will tell it to you if not I? Well, I'll tell it to you over and over again until you realize that in Europe the same thing is happening.

Let me draw an analogy. I have a rhododendron in a planter box beside my house. It's watered properly, it gets the proper amount of sun, and it's dying anyway. No matter what I do, it's dying. But in this fertile planter box, a weed has appeared. An errant seed has popped into the planter box and it's being starved, it's left to dry, yet this weed is growing. It's thriving. It's overtaking my rhododendron. And of course as a biologist, I studied survival of the fittest from my earliest days and I have to ask myself, what has happened in the planter box called America that we are being pushed out of our own planter box by invading weeds?

I know that's a harsh statement. I recognize that it will ruffle the feathers of all of those sensitive liberals who can't wait to be thrown off roofs by ISIS. I know it will really unsettle all of the feminists who cannot wait to be thrown down wells by the very people they embrace. I recognize that. But since they suffer from the mental illness called liberalism and I am a healthy, sane American male, I'll continue. And I will tell you that this country is dying because the American people have become weak.

Now, here are some headlines that caught my eye—printed stories: "New American Century: Arabic Is Fastest-Growing Language in USA," by Julia Hahn on Breitbart. From Breitbart again, "Le Pen: Europe's Migrant Flood Equals 'Barbarian Invasions of 4th Century.'" That's Marine Le Pen, the outspoken leader of France's National Front. From Fox News, "ISIS Touts Baby Boom as Key to Caliphate's Future." These seventh-century throwbacks are raping their way to a population explosion. The black-clad Nazi vermin are raping their way across the Middle East and procreating with the captured brides. Not one word from the American goddesses of feminism. ISIS women are being fed garbage such as "How to

Raise a Jihadi Baby." Then there's "Sister's Role in Jihad"—
which features a picture of an infant in a cradle lying next to
a pistol and a grenade. And in this country we have a smirker
in the White House who wants to take away your right to bear
arms.

Remember when National Rifle Association president
Charlton Heston told gun opponents they'd have to pry his
gun from his cold, dead hands? That should be our motto,
your motto. Never give up your weapon. Never give up your
weapon to one of the Nazis in this government. Never. It's
the only reason that ISIS will never take over this country.
It's because of an armed civilian population. It's the reason it
has been able to rampage across Europe, because the French
have been disarmed, the British have been disarmed. The
citizens of Europe are afraid of ISIS. But they won't be afraid
much longer. They won't be afraid much longer because the
revolution is brewing in Europe. Unfortunately for them, they
have no way to defend themselves other than with their fists
and their brains because the Obamas of Europe stole their
guns a long time ago—as they did in Australia, by the way.

That's another headline. How about one more? Obama
continues to push a new trade pact with some parts of Asia, not
including China. He's calling it the Trans-Pacific Partnership
trade deal. Why is this devious, anti-American leader doing
this? Is it good for American business? Well, it's good for some
of the traitors, some of the greediest, who would sell their
mothers' shoes if they could to get a bigger bottom line.

You have no idea what contempt I have for these people.
You have no idea what I would do if I had power. If you think

this is something I'm making up, I pity you. Do you think George W. Bush went to war in Iraq to free the Iraqis so they could flash a purple finger that told the world they had voted? No. Did we go to war in Iraq because there were supposed to be weapons of mass destruction? Again, no. We went to war to enrich Cheney's Halliburton cronies and their ilk, the industrial complex that was going to rebuild the country after the demise of Saddam.

How can you accept a nation in which there are business-men who would do deals that would further eviscerate our industrial capacity and send jobs to Asia? Why would you do that at a time like this, when employment is in such a bad state, when our economy is still shaky, when the government is printing money to prop up the economy? Why would you sell the country out to Japan, Thailand, Malaysia, and other countries in the Pacific Rim? Why is Obama doing that? Is it to help us? No. It's to help a few of the giant quislings who do business with those countries who care less about America than Obama does, if you can believe it—largely Silicon Valley and others, by the way—guys like Mark Zuckerberg, a man without a country. Despite his billions, in my opinion, he is a man without a country. He has no loyalty to the nation that gave him this fortune, and he epitomizes everything that is wrong with American business today.

I oppose this trade deal. I oppose it not because I oppose free trade but because there is no such thing as free trade with those nations. Don't let them fool you; they have tariffs on American goods, which will remain in place. The only difference is that we, the moronic nation, have let the shyster in the White House trick us into thinking it's free trade when in fact it is not free trade—it's bent trade. And if you think I'm wrong, why did the AFL-CIO oppose this trade deal? How come I, Michael Savage, the vociferous nationalist talk show host who is so offensive to all of the delicate, supposedly superior liberals—how is it that my opinion on this trade deal, which is really a traitors' deal, is also opposed by the AFL-CIO and your hero, Bernie Sanders, the soapbox orator from New York's Lower East Side?

Here's another one. We hear, "Donald Trump declares war on Obama trade. Time to send the real businessman to the White House to end this." Well, what is Trump really advocating? It's not a war. It's survival of the fittest. We used to be the fittest, and we will be again. Wherever you look, it's really no different than it was when Darwin first articulated the idea of survival of the fittest. Nothing's really changed except that in our country, the country itself—the government itself—seems to be targeting the most fit people in America and inhibiting them in any way it can, every way it can, whether it's a boy on a playground or an athlete on a football field. There seems to be an almost devious madness to inhibit the fittest and to make certain that the weakest thrive while the fittest die off. If that's not national suicide, please tell me what is. When a nation takes its masculine pride and attempts to deball it at every turn by drugging it, debasing it, inhibiting it, tell me how that nation can survive.

No nation in history has ever done to itself what this nation is doing to itself right now. There's no one who can disagree with me. No one. If they do, they're insane. When you see article after article telling people who are white to be ashamed of their race by people who claim not to be racist, if that's not insanity, tell me what is. When you see radical sick feminists attacking boys and saying that large muscles are a sign of aggressiveness, tell me that's not mental illness. Tell me what is going to be required to save this nation from self-destruction.

This is a nation deep in the throes of an illness. It would be too easy to call it a mental illness, which I've done since 2005: liberalism as a mental disorder. I've redefined the illness America's suffering from as an autoimmune disease. America is suffering the equivalent of political AIDS. It is an autoimmune disease in which a retrovirus has invaded the country and encrypted itself into the DNA of the nation, has replicated itself, and is destroying the nation from within. The virus is called the Democratic socialist party. That is the virus that has invaded this country, that is destroying the nation from within. Now, if you want more of it, go vote for Grandma. Go vote for Grandma if more social breakdown is what you want. That's what you're going to get. Where cop killers are invited to her White House as the police they killed are buried.

I realize that this is harsh rhetoric. I realize that it offends the sensibilities of the refined types in America who don't want to think of such things. But I can't help it, because that's the way I see things. That's how I see things from the point of view of a biologist and the point of view of, let's say, a political observer. Great Britain has just said no to the EU's demands that it take in hundreds of thousands more young Muslim refugees. Why are so many men being brought into the European nations? And who are the quislings in the European Union who want to flood Europe with young Muslim men? Why are they bringing the armies in? They think they'll spare them at the end?

The madness of liberalism has almost no bounds. You've heard me call it a mental disease, and it's that—and more. It's a suicidal cult. Liberalism itself is a religion, and it's a suicidal one—everywhere you turn. Jerry Brown signing a euthanasia bill and acting as though it's something wholesome and good for the people. We know what it is. It's a death cult. Jerry Brown is leading a death cult in the state of California, and, typically, progressives always hold up their madness as something progressive.

What can we, the people, do as we watch this going on? In the past we could sort of ignore it. But now when we see the waves upon waves upon waves of mostly young, virile men coming into Europe, and now we see a president trying to do the same thing to America and there's nobody stopping him—there's a bunch of old, weak, corrupt drunks on the Republican side—who's going to stop him? So he figures, "Why not do what I want to do?" That's why in one weekend he went from "We'll bring in 10,000 Syrians," to 100,000 on Saturday morning, to 200,000 on Sunday morning. The man was almost giddy. He was running it up the flagpole, as they used to say many years ago, to see what would happen. And guess what? There was scant opposition.

Where is the opposition? Ah, the people, you say? Except that we don't matter. We have no power. When did the people of a nation ever have power? Tell me that. Stop living in a fantasy world of the thirteen colonies. You know, what I don't understand is how people can compare a colonial system of the 1700s to today. It's a different universe. Maybe the same principles apply, but the same issues of governance don't apply. It just doesn't work when you have a multiethnic society at this point in history and a society of this size. So stop harkening back to Ben Franklin with the key and the lightning storm. We're not in the fifth grade. Those nonsensical comparisons don't work. They're academic.

Let's get down to brass tacks. What are we going to do about the situation? Survival of the fittest. There was a time in Great Britain when Neville Chamberlain, a quisling leader, was in power right after Germany invaded Poland. Do you remember what he said before that invasion? Chamberlain came back from a meeting with Hitler and said that he had in his hand an agreement guaranteeing that England and Germany would never go to war again. He guaranteed "peace for our time." Hip hip hooray. The next day Hitler invaded Czechoslovakia, and the citizens of Great Britain realized that Chamberlain was a suicidal Conservative who was going to destroy England. They needed a war leader. His own party voted him out. They replaced him with the great nationalist, Winston Churchill.

Remember the movie *The Godfather?*

Tom Hagen: "Mike, why am I out?"

Michael Corleone: "You're not a wartime consigliere. Things may get tough with the move we're trying. You're out, Tom."

Do you people not understand that sometimes art imitates life and teaches us lessons?

Neville Chamberlain was not a wartime consigliere. Germany was on the move. Hitler was invading. Hitler had built up his military even though they said he couldn't. And this weakling, this good-natured weakling, the pacifist, socialist intellectual, came back with an agreement that he couldn't wipe his nose with, as far as Hitler was concerned.

So his own party got rid of that quisling English leader. That's the benefit of a parliamentary system. We don't have such a system here. But somewhere deep within the controlling elements of this government are those who actually run things. God only knows who they are. I could probably give you a short list of those who I think are really running things, but I'm not completely sure who they are. But even they, at a certain point, recognize that a nation can be destroyed from within and they've gone too far by putting this maniac in the White House. The maniac has broken free of their controls just as others in history have done, others who were first put into power by more powerful people before going rogue on them.

It happened in Germany. It's not a direct comparison, but if you remember the history of Hitler, if you read about him, he didn't come to power on his own or in a vacuum. Very powerful industrialists backed him in the beginning. The Krupps, for example, who had been bankrupted after World War I. They were the main armaments manufacturer. They backed Hitler because they knew he'd be good for business. Dwight D. Eisenhower told us to beware the government military-industrial complex, right?

The same elements are present here in America. There are certain people who wanted Obama in. You know them: George Soros, John Kerry, Ted Kennedy, and the disgraced John Edwards. They figured they could always control him. And now he's gotten so crazy that he's gone off the reservation.

If you think Joe Biden was a potential savior, you're wrong and you ought to see your psychiatrist. Biden gave a speech about homophobia. At a time when ISIS is throwing gays off rooftops, burning churches, killing Christians, raping its way across the Middle East, that was all this mouthpiece could think of – homophobia?

I had a little thought about Biden, by the way. You know that he was not electable. His inane, off-the-cuff comments were deadly. They helped sink his own abortive campaigns. Mentally, he's not all there. He was never going to step in during the 2016 election if Grandma couldn't make it to the finish line. Do you want to know the only reason they are still warming him up in the bullpen? I can't finish this without risking a great deal. But I had a shocking thought. It's that the rogue president has broken free of his handlers. That's as far as I can go with that. The rogue president has gone so far to the left that his handlers may need someone to keep the nation from going completely down the drain. Of course, God help us if we've reached a point where Biden is a savior.

Which raises the question: Can his own party remove Barry now that he's gone rogue? Because he's getting more brazen by the day. He's gone way beyond anything he ever dreamed he would ever do to "transform" America. Everyone has a list of dreams. This guy has gone so far beyond everything he ever thought he could get away with that he's continuing down the path of such national destruction that it's now bordering on national suicide—even his own party sees that, probably within the Hillary camp. As much as I detest most of her policies, I've got to tell you something: she is actually more of a centrist than Obama is.

Don't get me wrong, I never supported her. I would never vote for her. Any Republican would have been better than Hillary Clinton except for Marco Rubio. I put an *X* through him early on. He's nothing but a shill. He's a shill for Larry Ellison and Silicon Valley. He's in favor of accepting the massive influx of immigrants without any controls. I mean, Rubio was a disaster, a walking, talking total disaster, in the Senate and on the campaign trail. Other than him, any Republican would have been better. But I'm not saying I'm supporting Hillary Clinton. Of course you can jump to that conclusion if you want. It doesn't matter to me what you want to jump to. But I think even within the Hillary camp there are rational billionaires who recognize that the nation is being destroyed from within and there's only so far that you can push people until they snap.

A final note: I keep saying "Hillary Clinton, Hillary Clinton" over and over because I can't just call her "Clinton." It would be too easy to confuse her with her husband. They're different people, even though their policies, corruption, and thievery would be the same.

THE INTERNET EXPOSES ISIS,
THE MODERN-DAY MONGOLS

Our complacency is not just about America as an idea defined by borders, language, and culture. It's also about America as a place with open cyberborders.

I want to explain how the barbarism of ISIS compares to that of the Mongols. The Mongols did almost exactly what ISIS is doing right now: they brutally and ruthlessly terrorized their neighbors.

Who were the Mongols? They came out of the north of China, and they were so vicious that they achieved a series of conquests that still have no parallel in human history.

The Mongols were a horde of nomadic horsemen who arose during the thirteenth century. They threw off Chinese rule and fused Turkish tribes into a loose military alliance. Led by Genghis Khan, the Mongols swept down from their central camp on the Onon River in Siberia and in 1215, after a three-year battle, took a great prize: Peking, now called Beijing. The Mongols slaughtered its inhabitants.

Then Genghis Khan went west and conquered western Turkestan, Persia, Armenia, and India. He slashed his way down to Lahore and south Russia. His bloody reach extended as far as Hungarian Silesia. He was such an effective monster that he built an empire that reached from the Pacific to the Dnieper River.

The Mongols took few prisoners. When they got into Hungary, for example, they killed or absorbed the Magyars, just as the Magyars had previously massacred and assimilated the Scythians and Avars and Huns. When the Mongols conquered, they massacred everybody who wouldn't fight alongside them. They killed everybody except the women they wanted to use as sex slaves.

Does this sound familiar? It's very similar to what you see going on with ISIS right now, with one difference: the Mongols had a bitter animosity toward Islam. They captured the city of Baghdad and slaughtered everyone—men, women, and children. Not only did they kill all the people, they destroyed the famed irrigation system that had kept Mesopotamia prosperous and populous from the early days of Sumaria. It was one of the most advanced irrigation systems the world had ever seen, bringing water to what is modern-day Iran, Iraq, and Syria—and the Mongols destroyed it. From that time on until very recently, Mesopotamia was a desert.

After the Mongols conquered and killed everyone, the eastern Mongols became Buddhists, like the Chinese. The western Mongols became Muslim. That's how the Muslims arrived in China. That is why, today, you see hundreds of indomitable Chinese fighting alongside ISIS. It's one of the best-kept secrets in the world.

The world has seen this type of barbaric behavior before, most notably by the Huns under the infamous Attila, who fought the Romans. It appeared more recently during World War II with the Japanese Rape of Nanking and the Japanese treatment of enemies and prisoners. That equaled or exceeded the barbarism of the Mongols.

Now we're facing new barbarians very much like the Mongols. They want to kill everyone in sight if they don't convert to their religion, if you want to call it a religion.

I understand that what these butchers are spewing is not classical Islam. If you say that all Muslims are terrorists, you are wrong. If you say that the terrorists' vision is a purist vision, that is also outrageously absurd, because raping eight-year-old girls is not my idea of purism. But if you say that ISIS can corrupt and infiltrate and transform parts of the world through a series of small attacks like those we are witnessing now, you are not wrong. It is a continuation of a long history of the same kind of bloody intimidation we've seen over and over. What happened in Paris, San Bernardino, and Orlando will continue to happen in America because of the weaklings we have running everything and because of the liars in the intelligence agencies. Even the brave men and women in the intelligence agencies have been hamstrung by Obama's left-wing insanities. They know what might happen. Instead of preemptively arresting terrorists and taking them in before they kill us, the maniacs in the Obama administration stick to their college-girl view, which is that it "wouldn't be our values"; it wouldn't be this, it wouldn't be that.

So it's inevitable that they're going to attack us again and again in this country before the people finally rise up and stop it themselves by electing someone like Donald Trump, who is a strong man, who will finally do what needs to be done to stop them.

You don't need to fear that ISIS is going take over and rule the world. It's not going to. There's a huge difference between ISIS and the small Arab armies of a thousand or less who, in their heyday before and during the Crusades, took over 50 percent of the world. In only a hundred years, those small bands of armies, in very much the same way as the ISIS terrorists, took over huge parts of the globe through the very same methods: terrorizing, raping, kidnapping, burning, destroying cities.

But there is a difference between then and now, and the difference is the very thing that ISIS members are using to communicate with one another, to conduct these atrocities. It's the Internet, and the Internet is what will be their downfall, because everyone now can see in an instant the vicious insanity of these throwbacks. In the past, people would have heard about it, but they wouldn't have really known about it, and they wouldn't have been prepared for them, nor would they have been ready to fight them. But now, the very same Internet the terrorists use to advance themselves and their perverse view of Islam will be used against them to destroy them. As more and more Americans arm themselves and learn marksmanship, the odds will go against these new barbarians among us.

When you see that Democrats have voted with Republicans to jointly sponsor a simple, commonsense measure that would increase the scrutiny of refugees coming from Iraq and Syria, you can see that even those dodos, the Democrats, understand that they'll be thrown out of office, because the people who elect them know what must be done.

ISIS is not the Mongols, unless we allow that to happen.

HOW TO WIN AT CYBERWARFARE

How can you stop ISIS unless you first stop its members from using Twitter and Facebook? How would *you* do it? That's a serious question. It's easy to say in a vacuum, "We don't want the government to interfere with the Internet." It's very nice, I'm sure the ACLU loves it, but we're way past that point. Not only do we have to control the Internet, we also have to use it effectively, create propaganda to smear ISIS and to make those terrorists look like the vermin they are.

I mentioned before that during World War II, the Germans and the Japanese were caricatured as the monsters they were, in terms of being our enemies. You saw it on posters, you saw it in movies, you heard it on the radio. The caricatures were done to turn those enemies into objects rather than people so that when our boys went out to fight them on a battlefield they would be better able to kill them rather than be killed by them. There were no left-wing political correctness police telling us "It's insensitive to all Japanese to depict their leader, Tojo, as a bucktoothed midget."

That's what war requires: anger, outrage, hate. We don't have any propaganda campaigns now, and we have an administration that's afraid even to say our enemies are Islamofascists. If we hope to beat them—and we better soon, or they'll be cutting off heads in your community—we have to define them as they are. They are subhumans. Do you understand that? They're lower than most animals. If you have a problem with that statement because you're a good liberal, tell me whether you consider raping an eight-year-old girl until she bleeds to death to be the behavior of a human being.

We heard testimony in Congress from a Yazidi—a religious Kurd—leader on what ISIS is actually doing on the ground. It's beyond a horror movie put out by Steven Spielberg. It's beyond anything that Stephen King could ever write, what those subhumans are doing. Take the worst thing you can imagine and magnify it to the nth degree of horror. That's what those people are doing to religious minorities, Christians, Yazidis. You tell me those creatures are human beings? Human beings have faces. Those animals hide them behind black masks, like the criminals they are.

When they do those horrible things on a regular basis— as a group, not an individual psychopath here and there, but an entire army some thirty thousand strong, doing them as a matter of course—that army and the culture that encourages them is subhuman. Trump said he would kill them and their families. What's wrong with that? What, do you think the families are sacred? Didn't you see it was a woman who led the San Bernardino terrorist attack? Is a woman, a wife, a mother sacred even if she wants to blow up your children in a day care center? Do you imagine that the husband of such a creature wouldn't know what was going on?

What's wrong with people on both sides, the murderers and the bleeding hearts, who see this happening and do nothing? I know what's wrong. The liberals are never going to change their misguided feelings of compassion for those who don't deserve it. They're not going to change in this lifetime, unless there's another 9/11, God forbid. If there were an attack ten times as big as 9/11, maybe they would wake up. But I don't think they will even then. They'll find a way to say we brought it on ourselves, we deserve it. That's what the infamous imam of the Ground Zero mosque implied after the attacks. That hypocrite, this smug Kuwaiti Feisal Abdul Rauf, who spearheaded the effort to build a mosque next to the World Trade Center site, said that our policies made us an "accessory" to the tragedy—which left liberals nodding in agreement, saying he was trying to build a bridge between Americans and Arabs. Only a handful of public figures such as Rudy Giuliani and Sarah Palin condemned the remarks.

I think the American people are so drugged, so overentertained, so distracted, that unless a bomb goes off under their feet they won't even care about it. I think we have become so atomized, separated, alienated from reality that it's almost impossible to wake up.

I'm not talking about the die-hard audience that listens to my show and reads books like this and knows what's going on. I'm saying that if you look around the streets, you see people who are zombies. They may look nice in a suit and tie or a nice dress and a pair of shoes, they may text while they walk and drive, but they're the living dead. They don't want to know what's going on, and anyone who says anything that requires any forcefulness, they consider those words and that speaker barbaric. They prefer the whispered monotones on NPR, those lunatics who brainwash listeners, who ravage them with mad leaders. They think that talking about the truth, as awful as it is, is barbaric, but looking for the good in those who are raping eight-year-old girls and then selling them into slavery isn't. How did the world get turned so upside down?

Yes, we must use a social media campaign and maximum measures to destroy ISIS, even if that means carpet bombing them and inflicting collateral damage. You can't pinpoint an ISIS member without killing family members as well, and sometimes that includes innocent people, unfortunately, because those subhumans surround themselves with innocent people. Ask the Israel Defense Forces what their experiences have been in fighting Hezbollah and others and how their enemies use human shields. How terrorists launch rockets from schools, mosques, or hospitals so they can accuse the Israelis of war crimes when they defend themselves by firing back. And then that toothless body of anti-Semites, the United Nations, eagerly endorses the terrorists' position. Enduring genocidal attacks, enduring the censure of Jew haters, but continuing to do what's right—that is what real warfare is all about.

But *we* are afraid to wage a counterattack on social media. The insanity has to stop.

Think about what I'm calling for as a kind of digital carpet bombing of portions of the Internet. We have to control it in order to stop ISIS from spreading its message of hatred. If you don't think the enemy is doing the same thing in Iran, in Syria, in Libya, in Yemen, shutting our voices out, you're delusional. Not just there but in other closed societies such as China, North Korea, even our new "friends" Cuba. Maybe you're afraid that once you permit an overbearing government to gain control over the information superhighway to such an extent, it could be used to control those among us who are the victims, rather than the perpetrators, of terrorism. This is a rational fear, given that power corrupts and absolute power corrupts absolutely. But I'm suggesting a policy in which Muslims who engage in terror, as well as the "friends" of those sick, murderous people, would not be able to use the Internet. Them. Not everyone. Target them by profiling them.

The liberals will say you can't do that because it's racial profiling. They will kick and scream and say you cannot have a ban on Arabic. They will cry like babies if you suggest that anyone who communicates on the Internet in Arabic will be shut down here and in participating countries. They will scream that if America actually insists on one language, one culture, it's profiling by linguistics. These are the same whiners who screamed that the new mayor of London, Sadiq Khan, wouldn't be allowed in Donald Trump's America because he's a Muslim. That misrepresents Trump's stated position, just as the arguments against an Internet crackdown misstate the extent of what is being suggested.

Okay, let's look at the flip side. If we do nothing, we are inviting the radical Islamists to blow up our nursery schools next time, our day care centers. And we can be proud of the fact that we're all good liberals and good First Amendment individuals, right? We'll all sign on to the suicidal notion that criticizing Muslims is hate speech, now banned by law.

Do you see the self-destructive insanity at work here? We have got to do something. We've got to start somewhere. We're doing nothing right now. Zero. We have Government Zero, as I wrote about in my previous book. We have Government Zero with President Zero. How can we begin to defend ourselves, except by denying the enemy access to our shores and our social media?

The information superhighway was created with federal funds. Taxpayer money created it. The companies controlling it are the robber barons of our time, individuals and corporations that stepped in, like the Internet wildcatters they are, and capitalized on the flow of oil, so to speak. It's time to get those robber barons to control the superhighway that was given to them just as they controlled the railroads that opened the West to settlers.

They already exert some control. Facebook users were able to paste a site-generated gay rainbow flag over their faces to support gay marriage, but they could not do the same to support the Confederate flag. Is that not censorship? Isn't Facebook already interfering with free speech? Mark Zuckerberg's little-girl minions took down pictures I posted on my Facebook account, pictures that showed what the Islamofascists were actually doing. They censored me. Why don't they censor the Islamofascists? Which side is Zuckerberg on?

We already know the answer to that. He's on the same side as the liberals who cheered the black woman who took it upon herself to break the law, climb a flagpole, and remove the Stars and Bars from the front of the South Carolina statehouse in 2015. Hillary Clinton hailed her as a hero. Breaking the law to fight the Confederacy, which was defeated before my grandparents were born—that's okay, but fighting a deadly modern enemy using all the tools at our disposal is not?

It's madness!

Trump has said that we should shut the Internet off in parts of the world, and he's 100 percent right about that. But I say we need to go further, much further, so here's an idea: not only should we target certain portions of the Internet throughout the world for a blackout of the Internet and turn it off completely, the government needs to begin a special quasi-military draft—not a generalized draft, because we don't need everyone—but a specialized selective service call-up of every computer-savvy young man and woman. They're never going to enlist in the military, so we need to draft them immediately using a targeted Selective Service draft. Just as we have targeted chemotherapeutic agents to fight specific illnesses, we need to target specific citizens for the Selective Service. We don't need 3 million to 4 million people to go onto the front lines. We need only a few thousand computer-savvy people to monitor, engage, corrupt, and destroy.

Actually, it doesn't matter what the age group is. Let's look at tech-savvy retirees. From age eighteen on, they need to be drafted into cyberdivisions of the US military, at some command post deep in the bowels of America, so they can do something useful for America. Then we may have a chance of defeating the Islamofascists.

You think this idea is too extreme? China already has a huge underground facility with young cybersavvy individuals who are on the Internet all the time trying to penetrate various aspects of our government and spy on us, hurt us, shut down our military computers, and otherwise weaken us. We have such divisions in our own military or we wouldn't even be functioning, but we don't have enough. We don't have a cyberarmy. We have a lot of generals in our intelligence services but too few foot soldiers.

Don't ask them if they want to join, force them to join. It doesn't matter how many lawyers they get, override the lawyers. It doesn't matter how many roads they try to block, tear gas and arrest them. It's about time we shut down anarchy the way we need to shut down the enemy. Eighteen years or up, you're going to be drafted if you're a computer expert or if you want to go to boot camp to learn to be a computer expert.

You're going to fight this war and Islamic fascism, and you're going to do it immediately, whether you want to or not. You're going to protect the homeland, your family, your sisters and girlfriends who are at risk of rape, slavery, and murder. Let me repeat in case you're still asleep: we're at war, they're at war, they're killing us, we're not fighting back the way we need to fight back.

The war is not just with the Islamofascists. It's not just with other nations. There are anarchists and subversives right here at home. Liberals would rather protect kids from God in school than from ISIS propaganda on the Internet. Let me rephrase that: they don't want the Judeo-Christian God in school. Allah would be okay, if some Muslim kid wants to pray. Can you imagine the public relations disaster you'd have if some Sunni kid was denied the right to pray when the Quran requires? But just try to mention God in the Pledge of Allegiance, you'll have so-called humanists screaming. Did you know that the courts decided that kids are no longer required to stand during the Pledge? Or even say it at all?

Any mention of the Judeo-Christian God is rooted out by the psychotics with law degrees in the terrorist organization called the ACLU, which attacks our fundamental liberties and our fundamental belief in God and says virtually nothing about the war on terror. Those misguided lunatics are actually on the other side. They're also brainwashing the young. You see millennials on the streets of every major city, with their wide uneducated eyes and clipboards clutched in painted fingernails—the boys have them, too—asking passers-by, "Do you have a moment to talk about human rights?"

These are a few of the little drones we should pick up, reeducate, and put into our new cyberarmy. We can also conscript some existing hackers. Some, but not all: too many of them have a criminal mind-set. I'm not saying they're criminals, but they definitely think like criminals. There are two different types, basically: hard hackers and soft hackers. A soft hacker will go in and look at people's stuff but won't change anything. A hard hacker goes in, changes stuff, and brings websites down, and does cyberdamage to the equipment or the place or the company or government or whatever.

Wait, you say, aren't most hackers left-wing fanatics? No, most hackers are just rebels. They just want to do hacking. In other words, a lot of them are renegades and somewhat criminal in their mentality.

But if you drafted them, wouldn't they be unmanageable? Wouldn't they get into ISIS bank accounts and steal the funds for themselves? They'd like to, sure. A few courts-martial and prison sentences would stop that, though maybe that could actually be an inducement: a share of the spoils instead of a Bronze Star. You have to know how to talk to them. Not as a computer-savvy person but as a rebel. Listen, I'm a rebellious person, as old as I am. I've been a rebel all my life. I rebel against any authority. Ask people who know me. Anyone tells me what to do, I bristle and go the other way.

You cannot appeal to a rebel to do the right thing; that's not going to happen. You have to position it as a challenge, not a command. It has to be something like "I dare you to break into ISIS's Internet, China's Internet, or Russia's Internet." They'll see it as a way to strut their stuff, to preen. Which is another way to get them to give this project their all. It's called motivation. They're always trying to find out who's the best. They're always trying to find out who can get whom. If you take a group of really good hackers and put them into the same room and say, "This is our challenge today," they're going to go against one another to try to see who can finish it first. You ever watch video gamers play in the old arcades? They had one eye on the screen, one eye on what the ace next to them was doing. That forced them to up their game. Those guys and gals might not care about our nation's security; they'd just like to solve the puzzle. They say the only reason they won't try to do certain stuff is that they are afraid of the criminal charges that would come against them. They don't trust the government, nor do I. It's an untrustworthy enterprise to begin with. We have the sneakiest president in the history of this country, one who is beneath contempt. We have to draft cybersoldiers, and then we have to tell them, "We are going to pay you this much money, and we'll write you a paper saying you're free of all charges against you for hacking in these areas."

This means immediately getting rid of the bureaucracy and legal issues. You want to write executive orders, Mr. President? Write that one. Write an order that frees the NSA, the National Security Agency, which has been forced to fight this urgent war with one hand tied behind its back. We—no, you—have done this to it because we have been bullied by a handful of liberals to be so concerned about civil liberties that we're in danger of losing both our civility and our liberties.

It's time to get off the seesaw. Let's get fully involved in this fight for survival. I've said it before, and I'll keep saying it: we have to get rid of the rules of engagement like those Obama has imposed upon our fighting men. For example, fighter pilots are coming back from sorties and saying they couldn't even drop their bomb loads because one of the girls in the sorority told them not to drop the bombs on a target in Iraq because we might do some collateral damage. The same thing is going on here. We are crippled by the communist mentality, the top-heavy bureaucracy that was established long before Obama but that has metastasized into a Frankenstein.

I have another suggestion on how to wrangle the hackers we so desperately need. I mentioned educating the drones: show them some of the beheading and murder videos that ISIS has posted. Show them the Syrian pilot being set on fire in a cage. Show them a small group of Arab men in a cage, slowly being lowered into water and drowned. Tell them that if they don't stop the subhumans who did that, they'll be suffering the same fate at the hand of a soulless enemy. After that? They'll be glad to break into ISIS networks. Patriotism may be a foreign concept to a lot of those people, but fear is universal. Scare them, and they will help. It's the same way we got rocket scientists to come onto our side after the fall of Nazi Germany. Those guys had a choice: come to America and work for us, or go to the USSR and live in a forced-labor camp. The ones who weren't captured and forced to work for Stalin chose to come here. Without the know-how they developed creating V2 rockets, it would have taken years longer to get into space. Ironically, without the space program we wouldn't have the satellites, microchips, and miniaturized cameras that make the Internet and cell phones possible. At least, they would have taken much longer to develop.

I think this plan would work because I understand hackers. I get along with them because we think the same way. Fundamentally, when you think about talk radio, if it's truly rebellious, it's actually hacking into the mentality of the country. I'm telling you, if we're good at talk radio, we're going up against the status quo and hacking the mainstream BS. In talk radio we say, "No, that's not what it is. We're going to take down that big lie, and we're going to tell you what we think the truth is." I suspect that a large number of individuals in the hacking community listen to the show because they think the same way. Even so, this is too critical to leave to chance. Which is why we can't just seek out brilliant people and ask them to do it. Some might come because, like the rocket scientists, they'd rather work for Uncle Sam than for Uncle Abdul. The rest? I would require them to do it.

Many of the people we need are already working for the buccaneers of the Internet fortunes. Notice I didn't call them entrepreneurs but buccaneers, corsairs. Mark Zuckerberg of Facebook, Bill Gates of Microsoft, Larry Ellison of Oracle, they're brilliant people, very successful. Those pirates have more money than they could ever spend during the next ten thousand years, yet they still want cheap labor. They push candidates who are for open borders, so they can bring in tech workers from India who will work for half the money an American worker will work for. This is how sickening their mind-set is. So they, too, would have to be forced to cooperate.

You see, those people who prospered in this land of opportunity are the reason we're losing technological superiority, why we need a cyberarmy, why we have to recruit and train our young. It's because the buccaneers of the superhighway pay politicians off. What do you think Obama does when he goes to Silicon Valley and gets $30,000 a head for a speech? Why do you think they organize these speeches for him? It's to keep him from demanding anything of them. It's cheap. They throw together a dinner somewhere at a hotel, they have an entertainer. Some guy comes along and does a song for them, and then they get to keep cashing in.

That's why Facebook and Twitter and Instagram aren't forced by the federal government to stop permitting the terrorists from using their highways. Obama may force mom-and-pop operations to support maternity leave, sick leave, a higher minimum wage, transgender bathrooms, and other crippling burdens. But when it comes to Silicon Valley, nothing. He goes there, he gives speeches, and Zuckerberg gets to do nothing for America except line his pockets with more profits. The same for Bill Gates, despite all of his PR agents saying what a nice guy he is: He is not using Microsoft to stop terrorists.

What would it take for Zuckerberg to shut down al-Qaeda access to one of his highways? How would he do that? I talked to a computer security expert. He said the issue is that it would be a little bit difficult. First off, ISIS would be able to use a VPN, a virtual private network. So you screen for those accounts. You have the Department of Defense, Department of Homeland Security, CIA, or whoever, whatever outfit you'd like, keep a liaison with you at corporate headquarters. They look through all posts in a given language: Farsi, Pashtun, Arabic. They look through posts in that given language, they run the algorithms the NSA already has, and they immediately delete and shut down accounts. It would be literally immediately, if you put the right amount of work into it, and it wouldn't be particularly expensive.

So why isn't Barry Obama's government doing this? It isn't just because of fund raising. That's when my security guy blew my mind. He said, "ISIS is useful. ISIS creates instability. ISIS keeps the Gulf States on their toes. They keep Syria on their toes because we want to build a pipeline to keep Syria under pressure."

Incredible. He was basically saying that the government is letting ISIS exist. It makes sense; we *could* shut it down. We bullied Facebook, Twitter, Verizon, we bullied any number of tech companies when we needed them to cooperate with then-legal NSA dragnet spy programs. Clearly this is guilt by omission, at least in my opinion. We have the power to take command and do something about this, but we haven't. The same President Obama who tells our Air Force not to bomb a convoy of oil trucks because the fires will pollute the environment, who tells them not to blow up pickup trucks during a victory parade, who tells Air Force pilots to come back with full bomb loads on bombing missions is telling people in cybersecurity to look the other way and let ISIS plot its next attack.

People in government tell me that they would love to get up and scream that they know what's going on, they could stop the next attack, but they're being prohibited from doing so by higher-ups. In its current iteration the war on terror is an absolute fraud. We watch Christians being crucified by ISIS while millennials are encouraged to post selfies on Instagram.

What's the endgame of Obama and his acolytes? What do they want, the enemy within? What are they doing? If Obama is really trying to sow the seeds of a Hillary Clinton presidency, what does he think the resulting garden will look like?

For the answer, look at the European Union. Look at its leaders. They long ago stopped caring about the will or the well-being of their people. It was only when the people of the United Kingdom took over and voted in a referendum that they started to notice—and the prime minister, David Cameron, didn't think the vote would succeed, which was the only reason he agreed to hold it. Now he's gone and Theresa May is in.

First things first. We have to understand that our government has betrayed us and has been betraying us consistently for over a decade. Our government does not represent our interests. It represents certain other interests. For the government, instability in the Middle East is a good thing. It keeps the Saudis buying weapons, it keeps them distracted from the Israelis. It keeps the Sunnis and the Shiites at each other's throats. ISIS is still handled with kid gloves by the Gulf States because they're concerned about an ultimate showdown with Iran, the growing Shiite power. They're concerned about that, but they see ISIS as a potential tool in the struggle. Iran has been very successful. Donald Trump himself said, "If Iran was a stock, I'd buy it yesterday," and he's right. It has been extremely successful with all of its efforts in the Middle East.

If we had a legitimate government, officials wouldn't be allowed to take money from the Zuckerbergs who have capitalized on the superhighways, they wouldn't be allowed to take money for their election campaigns. If they didn't take money, they could force the buccaneers to do the right thing. We wouldn't have to watch ISIS and al-Qaeda rule the cyberwaves like Britannia once ruled the sea. They would suggest their own operations to take down ISIS websites, al-Qaeda websites. The movie studios did that during World War II. The Zanucks and Warners and their kind were patriots. They were happy, willing, eager to make propaganda films to take down the Nazis, the Italian Fascists, the Japanese. I remind you of men such as David Sarnoff, whose name has probably been forgotten by now. Sarnoff owned NBC. He was either the general manager or the owner. He enlisted in the military as a colonel for $1 a year to lend his brilliance in organization and planning as a businessman to the war effort to defeat Germany and Japan. He was one of many great men in American industry who actually enlisted in the military at $1 a year in order to defeat Hitler.

Now tell me why Bill Gates hasn't enlisted in the military to defeat ISIS? Tell me why Zuckerberg hasn't enlisted any of his company to defeat ISIS? I'll tell you where I'd start. I'd force Zuckerberg to give up a certain percentage of his workforce for the military effort. And I'd make him pay for it. Good wages, top wages. What would be wrong with that idea? Didn't ordinary Americans scrimp and budget in order to buy war bonds during World War II? What would be wrong with Zuckerberg having to pay back this nation instead of catering to China? Are you going to tell me Facebook can't afford it? Are you going to say the shareholders would complain? Show them ISIS videos at their annual meeting. Until the enemy is destroyed, they'll shut up, I promise you. The same goes for Larry Ellison, and the same goes for Bill Gates. And the Google potentates. It's time for them to give back to this country.

Now, a lot of the people who work at Facebook, Google, Oracle, and Microsoft, aren't hackers. They are programmers. Hackers and programmers are two different animals. We need both. We need hackers to break into the ISIS and al-Qaeda websites or communications networks, and we need computer programmers to put out positive propaganda for young people in this country. We need those programmers to program positive information for the youth of America, to make them love their country again and want to help it. We'd have them take down the hyphenates, the "African" Americans, the "Muslim" Americans, the "gay" Americans and make us all what we were: Americans, who put flag above diversity. If we'd do that, we'd be involved in a cyberwar we might win. Until that happens, we're not going to win this war, we're going to continue losing it. And not slowly, but with increasing rapidity. Wait until virtual reality becomes commercialized over the next few years, when ISIS can recruit vulnerable kids with macho training, images of abuse of women, rape, and murder. Kids raised on video games will make a natural segue into something that current labeling and limitations prohibit. Imagine playing a game and then being told you can do that for real—not in Iraq, not in Syria, but in your own community.

It's coming, if we don't act now.

If we no longer have patriots at the level of a Sarnoff, we will have to force patriotism upon our population. If we can't get hackers who are patriots, we need citizens who aren't hackers to become hackers. They have to be tempted with access to technology they can only dream of, but they also have to be ethical—or at least ethical enough. I believe that when they start to see results, they may actually develop compassion, pride of country. But they also have to understand that the apparatus they will use to do their hacking requires access to systems at the top secret and sensitive compartmented information levels. What we would have to do is get all those thousands of people we're talking about to be trustworthy enough to handle TS/SCI data. Not all of them can be put into basements or caves like Cheyenne Mountain in Colorado Springs, where NORAD is located.

If we're going to do a selective Selective Service, we need to be very selective of who we select. They have to be patriots first because of the systems that they have to be given access to. You're basically introducing a bunch of potential Edward Snowdens. Snowden was very intelligent, but he was a grave detriment to our nation.

So the first ones we recruit have to be cybersavvy people who are also patriots. The tide in this country is turning to conservatism, patriotism, and national security. Those inspiring young minds should be put in the forefront of the cyberwar against ISIS. But we can't just give up on getting the hackers.

How do we stop a Snowden from undermining the war effort if he were recruited? There's a very simple answer to that, and that's very severe punishment: The death penalty if you wind up doing something against the war effort, or let's say twenty-five years in Fort Leavenworth. Nobody wants to go to Fort Leavenworth for twenty-five years. We tell our recruits, "You're free to hack. No punishment for that. But betray this nation, and your life is over."

That's how we deal with cyber-ISIS, with cybersecurity, and with cyberthreats to our nation in general. Because whether they come from China, whether they come from ISIS, ISIL, whether they come from insiders, these are probably the biggest, most dangerous threats to our nation since the creation of the atom bomb. The reason I say that is that cybersecurity isn't geographically located. With atomic bombs, you drop something on Nagasaki or Hiroshima and it's located to that area. A hacker can operate from anywhere and strike anywhere.

There's also a mind-set that needs to be overcome, the same one that has plagued and hampered our conventional warfare hand. Because of the nature of the cyberworld, as entities such as the National Security Agency, the Cyber Security Summit, or the US Cyber Command cast their nets out to do their work, it's inevitable that collateral damage will impact the innocent. The day is going to come, once ISIS bombs a few child care centers, a few disability centers, once they blow up a few more people around the country, that we're going to have to take the gloves off about stopping recruitment and radicalization on these shores. Meaning that if we take down the computers that control the terrorists' finances, their oil, their social media, other institutions may be hurt. For example, the banks that hold their billions. Even during World War II, far too many Allied banks were involved in the business of handling Nazi funds, making them grow. Americans were prolonging a war that killed Americans. We have learned nothing from history, and we are doing that again.

We are way past the point of optional, my friends. We're at war. Did you hear me? The terrorists know it, but we don't know it. They've been at war with us for a very long time. I will tell you right now, they are winning the cyberwar. They are certainly winning the propaganda war, which revolves around the cyberdomain and also around programmers.

Do you know the astonishing history of the Arabs? How in twenty-five years after the death of Muhammad they conquered so much territory through warfare, hatred, murder, racism, genocide. After only twenty-five years, Muslim power grew astonishingly using the same methodology that they're using now. Only now they have more power at their fingertips. Now they have explosives and the Internet. Think about what they did in twenty-five years using just sword and flame, rape and murder. Now there are the same psychotic mind-set, the same genocidal maniacs, generations later, and now they have TNT and the Internet to help them.

Think about what I'm saying, and you'll understand the danger we are in. You'll understand that we are in a war for our survival. You'll understand that we have a man in the leadership position called Barry Obama, who most Americans who have a rational brain know is intentionally not doing a sufficient job to defeat ISIS, which is why he was forced to give a speech about how fabulous his war is. We all know it's a lie. We all know he's a tin soldier, and we don't have to ask why. We don't have to ask how. I've addressed that elsewhere in this book. The only question is, when is this going to change? When are we going to get serious at fighting back? When are we going to stop ISIS from using cyberwarfare to defeat us and to convert this nation to a nation of slaves who follow their psychotic sharia law?

Back to our new, expanded cyberarmy. Not only do we have to conscript, we have to have an absolute draft without exemptions. No 4Fs. No conscientious objectors. They serve, or they go to prison. The minute you allow exemptions, there are going to be deferments for people who work for cybercompanies. I can guarantee you there will be a cyberdeferment that will be put into place, because Zuckerberg and Gates will lobby the president of the United States of America and some key senators on some stupid committee and say, "We need a deferment for our workers, because we are already working in a very important area, important for the American economy, we need them to be exempt from the draft."

You know that that's what they would do. There's no end to greed. The first thing you have to understand is that there's larceny in the hearts of most men. That's an old statement. As rich as those men are, there's not enough money on the planet for them. They'll do whatever they have to do to make more. Their machine will do anything it has to do to make certain that their profits go up, not down. It's that simple.

You might ask, can't you just put out an ad? That's naive. I spoke to the head of a tech company in Tennessee. The company had put out an ad looking for people. It needed coders. It pays relatively well, offers benefits. It's a proper job. It's got good pay for the region, higher than the median pay in the region, yet it had no takers from the United States. Then the company put out this job, and it also listed it as a freelance job. It got well over a hundred replies from India, decoding companies, individuals looking to freelance from Mexico, the Philippines, India, Malaysia, people from all over looking to program for it. But it got no responses from the United States.

The people who actually make the magic happen, the coders, the programmers, they're superb people. They have their noses to the grindstone, they're among the best workers in the world. The problem is that we don't turn out enough of them, and the jobs get taken by overseas workers. If we were to institute some kind of cyberdefense draft, it would give people a lot of experience. When they came out of the military, they would be better employees. They'd be the best.

Let's be even more ambitious. Let's create an ROTC, an officers' training center on campus, but at the junior high school or even elementary school level. In fact, we should create federal cyberschools—five or six of them across the United States that would be run by people from Microsoft, Facebook, and Twitter. They'd be drafted to run the schools in this time of war, and they'd set them up. Maybe the billionaires who own them would continue to pay them their same salary, since they've gotten so much from America for so little. Maybe they would continue to pay these guys great salaries, they could run those schools, and then we could attract young kids who might have the capacity for it. How long would it take a bright young American high school student who's computer savvy to be useful?

Less than a year. They don't need a university education per se. They don't have to learn how to put a condom on a cucumber at Harvard. You could take a bright, computer-savvy high school student, send him or her to a crash program, and within one year he or she would be useful to American companies.

Would that one year be about the same amount of time necessary for them to go to work for the government? To start taking down ISIS websites? No. For cyberwarfare they'd have to cut their teeth a little bit first, but it wouldn't be much more difficult. ISIS websites are mostly publicly hosted. ISIS is using social media whose companies are based in the United States. They're using Facebook, they're using Twitter, they're using Instagram.

We should be looking at Israel for the answer. I'm a supporter of Israel for obvious reasons: it is not just the only democracy in the Middle East, it does not just have the only prosperous society in the region, but it represents heroic stability in a sea of terrorists and poverty inflicted by greedy royal families. The Israelis are brilliant, but more than that they are what I wish Americans could be when dealing with their enemies: ruthless and subversive. They give no quarter, and they ask none. They are brutally effective at pursuing the interests of their people. That's what gets so many leftists riled up about Israel: they say, "How terrible, how terrible," because Israelis don't play the internationalist game. They just don't.

Of course, Israel's a sovereign nation with a national identity, and of course that's anathema to the new world order. Why is Israel not engaged in fighting ISIS, is what I keep asking. The answer is, why would you fight someone that's got literally all of your enemies all tied up into knots and not paying attention to you?

So we can't count on Israel for this, but we can learn from the fact that it has mandatory military service. We don't need that. We still have a sufficient number of patriots who want to serve, who want to become soldiers, who want to become SEALs. But we absolutely need mandatory cyberwarfare service, because we are losing that war. Like the war on the ground, that is something we cannot afford to do.

BRING BACK HUAC—CALL IT LAC (LOVE AMERICA COMMITTEE)

If Donald Trump becomes president, I wonder whether we'll see a revival of groups such as the House Un-American Activities Committee. I hope so. I can name several people who should go before HUAC today.

Some will say, "Well, come on now, that's fascistic." Really? You mean what the present administration and its anarchistic supporters is doing is *not* fascistic? You mean the controlling of our speech through boycotts and through false righteous indignation and control of the media is not fascistic?

This country needs a thorough housecleaning. And the new House of Representatives, once it's formed, should immediately consider House Un-American Activities Committee hearings.

We have people who stay in the government no matter who is in power. Republican president, Democrat president, these people are permanently fixed in places such as the State Department, and they do not fight for America. I'd like to know exactly what they're fighting for, other than themselves.

The number one person on the list of witnesses to call would be Barack Obama. His anti-Americanism has been exhibited by almost all of his activities since he became president. Number two on the list would be John Kerry, who lied about the Iran deal to sell it. He lied that US officials were dealing with moderates in Iran, when he knew all along that the Iranians have no moderates. The skilled storyteller duped America into passing the Iran deal.

Then there's Ben Rhodes, President Obama's foreign policy lying sack of guru. Rhodes bragged about how he had helped create the false narrative that said US officials were dealing with moderates in the Islamic theocracy, because the public would not have accepted the deal had it known that Iranian hard-liners were still calling the shots. Well, let me tell you something, Benny boy, I'm part of the public, and I knew you were a liar. Just like your boss, who has been a liar since the first day he could move his tongue.

The White House line, which Rhodes says he created, was that Obama started negotiations after the supposedly moderate Iranian president, Hassan Rouhani, was elected in 2013. Obama had set his sights on working out a deal with the mad mullahs as early as 2008. You mean he came into office to do the deal? Now you got the rest of the story. He was handpicked to do the deal.

Where did this unknown ghost come from? This man, this administration, was handpicked by foreign powers that manipulated him into the presidency. Because of the liars in the media, he has been able to get away with virtual murder. The murder of the truth, the murder of our national security.

I know many lives were, let us say, seriously challenged during the HUAC hearings of the McCarthy era, but I want to ask you something. Have you read the Venona papers? The Soviet-era secret correspondence that came out a little over two decades ago, which confirmed that almost everything that Joseph McCarthy had been saying about the news media and Hollywood was true? That there *were* communists who were openly subverting America?

Can anyone tell me the name of someone whose life was actually ruined by HUAC who was *not* really working to subvert America, who was not really a communist or fellow traveler? I'd like to know whose life was ruined. I think it's a myth that lives of innocent people were ruined. I know there were movies made, I remember *The Front* with Zero Mostel, in which he played an innocent actor who jumped out of a window because the House Un-American Activities Committee was after him. Hollywood has made many, many movies about the blacklist. We hear about the blacklist. But how many innocent people's lives were actually ruined? The operative word here is *innocent*. I'd like to know their names.

The House Un-American Activities Committee was an investigative committee formed by the U.S. House of Representatives. It was originally created—most people don't know this—in 1938 to uncover citizens with Nazi ties inside the United States, as well as possible Communist Party infiltrators. Now, if I were to revitalize and to suggest that we have a new HUAC, I would investigate people with Islamist ties inside the United States. Who would object to that?

I believe there are many traitors among us, such as the nuclear-secret thieves Julius and Ethel Rosenberg, people who would gladly see a dirty bomb go off in this country, and I stand by those words. We do not have the time. The time bomb is ticking, the Islamists are everywhere in this country, from the highest offices in the land all the way down to the local street level. How do I know that? Because the FBI told us that six months ago. They have more than a thousand active investigations, and they can't arrest those people. They have to let them kill somebody before they can even look at them.

Take a look at what happened in San Bernardino, California, and Orlando. The terrorists were on a watch list and the FBI could not stop them because we're all so intimidated by the human rights lawyers who are going to kill us all. I think it's long overdue that we have an investigation before the dirty bomb goes off, not after it. I know that it's an insensitive suggestion. I know it will rankle all of the sniffing liberal politicians in the corridors of power. How dare that loudmouth talk show host suggest such a barbaric thing as a new HUAC? Well, they are the very people who have brought us to this point of almost no return.

I'll remind you of something. Julius and Ethel Rosenberg were American citizens who were tried for, convicted of, and executed for conspiracy to commit espionage. Were they innocent? No. They were instrumental in passing information about the atomic bomb to the Soviet Union of Josef Stalin, which speeded the development of Soviet nuclear weapons. They were *disastrous* longtime communists and spies. Those American citizens, by the way, were tried as a result of investigations, and they were convicted of conspiracy to commit espionage in 1951 and put to death in the electric chair in 1953. There were many people who said they were not innocent. Many stories came out afterward by relatives and others, proving beyond a reasonable doubt that they were spies.

And they were surrounded by spies. Take Ethel's brother, David Greenglass, who supplied documents to Julius from Los Alamos and who spent ten years behind bars. He was absolutely guilty. There was Harry Gold, Greenglass's courier, who served fifteen years in federal prison. Guilty. There was also a German scientist named Klaus Fuchs, who turned over secret atomic bomb information to the Soviet Union and who served nine years and four months in prison. Guilty.

Now, this is the most important part of this little diversion. In 1995, the US government released a series of decoded Soviet cables code-named Venona. I had it on my radio show, the Venona papers, back in 1995. Those papers confirmed that Julius Rosenberg had acted as a courier and recruiter for the Soviets.

Ethel Rosenberg's brother, David Greenglass, whose testimony had condemned her, later stated that he had lied about his sister to protect his own wife, Ruth, who had been the typist of the classified documents he stole, and that he had been encouraged to do so by the prosecution itself. Morton Sobell, who was tried with the Rosenbergs, served seventeen years and nine months of a thirty-year sentence. In 2008, Sobell admitted he had been a spy and stated that Julius Rosenberg had spied for the Soviets and that Ethel Rosenberg had known what he was doing. There's a lot more to this story. Just remember that Julius and Ethel Rosenberg–type infiltrators are still alive and well, working like thieves in the night to undermine the pillars of our nation. We must root them out!

Back to what I asked a moment ago, a very, very straightforward question. Which of the actors, writers, and directors who were blacklisted were not, in fact, members of the Communist Party USA at the time or, let us say, secretly associated with communist parties at that time?

Let's hear about the current blacklist. As I said, HUAC was actually formed in 1938 to uncover those in America with Nazi ties, Nazi associations, as well as communists. There was no outcry in America then. Why was there such an outcry in Hollywood and the media when it increased its focus on communists? Well, the answer is that the communists had infiltrated Hollywood and the media deeply, according to the Venona papers.

This is why I suggest that we need to create a new HUAC in an attempt to ferret out those with Islamist ties in this country. What would be an Islamist tie? What does that mean? What would a congressional committee be seeking to discover in people they call before the new House Un-American Activities Committee? You'd have to change the name for the liberals, or the media would go insane. You'd have to call it something different, such as the Love America Committee. You know, use their tactics. The Love America Committee, the new LAC, would be seeking to find the Islamists and their sister travelers in the national security agencies, the Secret Service, the FBI, you name it.

People will say, "Look at history. Look at the Great Depression, capitalism wasn't doing too well. Capitalism wasn't meeting the needs of the people, so they were looking for something new." I would remind them that there's a saying, "The road to Hell is paved with good intentions."

Anyway, this is not about economics. This is about saving lives, investigating organizations and people who may have deep ties to Islamist front groups, finding out who is fronting for those who want to introduce sharia law into America, under which homosexuals would be killed and women put into burkas. That is an un-American idea?

Of course not. Have you ever looked at the Council on American-Islamic Relations or any of the other Islamist front groups in this country? If you actually read the literature, you will find out that there are quite a few groups that have openly espoused taking us back five hundred years.

This is not about suppressing ideas, either. This is about finding people who want to kill us and putting them into prison. I'd like to find out who the Islamists are in our intelligence agencies who are crippling our military and police. What is wrong with that idea? Why is it that our men can't go to war and kill the enemy without wondering if they're going to be arrested when they come back from the battlefield? Is that a way to fight a war? It's why we're not winning. Because Obama has crippled the military with his rules of engagement. Just as he has intimidated the local police across America, making them vulnerable to being attacked and killed.

I have raised hundreds of thousands of dollars for US marines who were court-martialed for things they didn't do on the battlefield, because they fired a little too quickly and killed the enemy before getting killed. I can cite one case after another of US marines who were imprisoned for being a little too good as warriors and not getting themselves killed or maimed first. We cannot let fear—the fear of uncovering those who are working in the halls of Congress—undermine both our international and our domestic security.

I ask again: Which innocent individuals were destroyed by HUAC? Search Google, and what pops up is an answer from, of all places, the Spartacus League. The Spartacus League is one of the most radical communist organizations in the United States of America. The Spartacus educational website has the most to say against HUAC. That should tell you an awful lot right there about the blacklist. When you read the site, you'll see why the Spartacus League fears the return of a HUAC-like organization. Its members would be exposed as subversives and find themselves first in line for the revitalized hearings.

Let's put that aside for a minute. The Alien Registration Act was passed by Congress on June 29, 1940. It made it illegal for anyone in the United States to advocate, abet, or teach the desirability of overthrowing the government. The law also required all alien residents in the United States over fourteen years of age to file a comprehensive statement of their personal and occupational status and a record of their political beliefs. According to the Spartacus League, the main objective of the Alien Registration Act was to undermine the Communist Party USA and other left-wing political groups in the United States.

Now, as I said, the House Un-American Activities Committee was originally set up by Congress in 1938 to investigate people suspected of aiding and abetting the Nazis, as well as uncovering communist infiltration, but the radicals in the Spartacus League—in other words, the Bernie Sanders types—leave that first part out of their discussion.

Then we go into the motion picture industry. HUAC named a number of individuals, Bertolt Brecht, names you wouldn't remember, Dalton Trumbo, Ring Lardner, Jr. They refused to answer any questions, and they were known as the Hollywood Ten. They claimed that the Fifth Amendment of the US Constitution gave them the right to do so, and they were right. That's why so many members of Obama's administration have copped to the First Amendment, and, like gangsters, have taken the Fifth. Have you ever lived through a time when the people who ran the IRS were under investigation for crimes against innocent civilians and would take the Fifth Amendment instead of answering questions and not be put in jail? That's what happened under your hero of liberalism, Barack Obama: they took the Fifth Amendment.

Do you know how many members of Obama's administration have gone before Congress? Not to investigate their, let us say, sympathies with organizations that would undermine America but to investigate their actual activities against innocent Americans, and they hide behind the Fifth Amendment. Yet nothing has happened to them. They could have been found guilty of contempt of Congress, and they could have been sentenced to six to twelve months in prison, but the spineless, plastic conservatives in the Republican Party did not do this.

Many of you will say, "Look, Mike, you don't believe in a blacklist, do you? You don't want one, right?" I'll answer that I wish it weren't necessary, but you're damn right I want one. I want one for people who hate our nation and want to see it destroyed. I want to know exactly who they are, and I want them stopped.

My colleagues, if they bother to read this at all, will sit there and say that such a thing is wrong. Unconstitutional. Inhuman. Is it? Well, how come none of you would-be defenders of truth and justice have rushed to my defense since I've been blacklisted by Fox, CNN, and all the major channels? How come you don't care about that blacklist? How come you don't care, all of you plastic conservative pundits out there, that I'm the only member of the American media banned from entering Great Britain for statements I didn't even make? Where were you when I needed you?

The answer is nowhere, because you're the very same plastic conservatives that you blast every day on television and in your writings.

9

OUR FUTURE

THE COMING ECONOMIC COLLAPSE?

The political class is obsessed with virtually every belch that goes on during a presidential campaign, and those within it can talk about a single belch for days—the exception being that the criticisms they have about Donald Trump, such as his hair, his spray tan, his fund raising—are all off limits where Hillary is concerned because then it would be antifeminist. I have always said it's much ado about nothing. During the most recent presidential primaries, our choices came down to one from column A, between a commie and a criminal—those would be Sanders and Clinton of the Democrats—or one from column B, between a showman and what the Yiddish call a *shande*—a shame. Those would be Trump and Ted Cruz of the Republocrats. Much ado about nothing.

During the mental abuse we endured during the endless primary season—and it was considerable—I took a break from politics for a day and watched a movie, *The Big Short*, which was about the collapse of our economy in 2007. The implosion was orchestrated by Wall Street—mainly the short sellers—and the movie was all about credit defaults for swaps where they had aggregated mortgages into big funds and then bet against them. It's an amazing film but very complicated.

Now, I'm pretty good at statistics. I'm not good at high finance. I am very good at low finance. As a kid, I would work in a luncheonette, make $9 or something for cleaning dishes all night, and then go home, do my homework late, go to school, and put the money in the bank. I liked having a little bank account. That's how I was. I was raised to save money. I come from a lower-middle-class-background, immigrant family. My folks were not that worldly. They didn't know high finance. It doesn't mean that they had great virtue for not knowing. There's virtue in knowing how to manage wealth, and there are some very virtuous wealthy people. There are people who just have a mind for this kind of thing, and they're not all crooks. I have a doctorate that included studying epidemiology statistics, and I could hardly follow the financial twists and turns in the movie. The person I saw the movie with is the CFO of a multibillion-dollar company, and even he had trouble following the plot.

But it's important that you see this film, not just to see how it all played out, how it was all resolved. It turned out not to be a break from politics at all, since the events portrayed in that film helped elect Obama. You should pay very close attention because it's happening again. I'll get back to that in a moment.

The movie is based on a book called *The Big Short: Inside the Doomsday Machine* by Michael Lewis. The book traces the roots of the global market collapse through the eyes of those who saw it coming and figured out ways to profit from it. First out of the gate was Dr. Michael Burry, the hedge fund manager who invented the credit default swap. Dr. Burry is an eccentric ex-physician turned one-eyed capital hedge fund manager, a stock-picking shaman who had one glass eye and an utter lack of social graces but who was able to crunch numbers while running around his office barefoot. He's sort of a hippie doctor. He wears shorts in his office. He goes to Supercuts for haircuts—my kind of guy. Christian Bale was fantastic in the part.

In the movie, Dr. Burry believes that the US housing market is built on a bubble that will burst in the next few years. The company he works for as an investor allows him to do virtually anything he pleases with its funds. Dr. Burry proceeds to bet against the housing market with the banks, and the banks, of course, are very happy to accept his proposal for something that has never happened in US history. The banks, you see, believe the doctor's a crackpot, and therefore they are confident that they will win the deal.

The doctor goes through the thousands of individual mortgages that made up the securities that underwrote so much of the banking industry. Though bankers thought they were solid because no one ever defaults on a mortgage, Dr. Burry realized that a dangerous number of subprime home loans were on the verge of going south, and he decided to plug more than $1 billion of investors' money into credit default swaps.

What he effectively did was bet against the housing market. In the movie we see him go to investment banks such as Goldman Sachs, and they think he's nuts. They say, "Well, how are you going to bet against it? There's no way to do it." He comes up with a thing called a credit default swap. The investment bankers say, "Sure, we'll take your money," because they feel that mortgages are never going to collapse. People pay their mortgages, right? But Dr. Burry has studied the individual mortgages and seen that people were already bailing in 2005. They couldn't make their mortgage payments. It's a fantastic story, but you need a head for business and you need to be an investor to really understand it.

During the housing crash, collateralized debt obligations were raging out of control and someone was trying to blow the whistle on Dr. Burry. During the Bernie Madoff period, someone was trying to blow the whistle on Dr. Burry again. The Securities and Exchange Commission (SEC) did nothing under Christopher Cox, who used to work for President Reagan. Cox was a seventeen-year Republican member of the House of Representatives, a White House staff member in the Reagan administration, a fine man in many ways. But he was also the twenty-eighth chairman of the SEC; he served from 2005 to 2009, which was exactly during the period that the housing bubble was created and crashed out the houses. Cox was succeeded by Mary Schapiro, another one who let it all happen, who looked the other way, who wouldn't listen to the whistle-blowers.

It's amazing to watch what goes on at Goldman as played in the movie. I'm not going to tell you the rest of the story because it would get too complex, but I'm recommending that you watch *The Big Short* if you want to see how it gave us the bane of Barack Obama. It recreates the environment of fear and mistrust that allowed voters to embrace someone they *thought* they could trust, someone who turned out to be just another fraud in an expensive suit.

Maybe it was the movie or maybe I'm just fascinated by the psychology of evil on a grand scale, but the day after I watched *The Big Short* I watched an interview with the fraud artist Bernie Madoff on ABC. Normally, I don't watch network television. I don't like ads, so I don't watch it. But I watched because I find Madoff compelling for a number of reasons: how he got away with his Ponzi scheme; the corruption and collusion with the SEC (meaning the Bush government at the time). And there was Chris Cox—blond-haired, blue-eyed Chris Cox, the head of the SEC. In my opinion, Cox should have gone to jail for having allowed Madoff to get away with what he did. Many people knew what Madoff was doing and knew he was a crook. They tried to blow the whistle on him, but the SEC looked the other way.

This hero out in Boston, Harry Markopolos, was the one who pursued it. Markopolos said that when he went to the SEC in Boston and tried to blow the whistle on what Madoff was doing, the people there laughed at him. He said, "Look, I'm a soldier. I'm an ex–military guy." So what? People didn't see why that made him so hot under the collar. He said, "I took an oath to defend America and the Constitution. This man is a criminal. What he is doing, hundreds of thousands of people are going to be destroyed by him." The SEC still looked the other way.

Madoff is an old story, but it's a new story, too, because—like the financial collapse that began in 2007—it's coming back again. There are many Madoffs running around America taking your money today. And a few Madoffs who still have it.

For example, I want to know why his wife, Ruth Madoff, is not in prison. Am I wrong in asking that? You know, we have weird laws in America. If, let's say, you're a criminal kingpin, you get arrested and go to prison, your wife has immunity from prosecution. Why is that? Is she the gentler sex? She didn't ride around in his limousines? She didn't fly in a private plane? She didn't go on his yacht? She didn't live in the big penthouse? She didn't eat like a queen in the apartment? She didn't pour $1,000 bottles of wine as it was all going down? Why is Ruth Madoff living out of prison in Connecticut? Why did the government—the corrupt government—allow her to take $2.5 million and call it a pittance of what she'd had? She should have been left with nothing. She lived on stolen money and ruined lives.

There's more to this story than meets the eye. Where did all those missing billions go? I'll tell you where one of the billions went—to the crooked lawyer who was appointed the trustee of all of the people who are making claims. He should also be in prison, in my opinion. This corrupt lawyer took a billion dollars in fees. This thief who was appointed to be the executor or whatever they call it, this overseer of all of the stolen money, this crook has taken a billion dollars in legal fees. You want to see a corrupt system? There's a corrupt system.

It's going to happen again. The housing bubble was built upon a house of cards and fraud. That's not a revelation. What the investors and bankers did was to change the name of the game from CDOs to the newly invented BTOs—bespoke tranche opportunities—which is just Wall Street language. What does it mean? The same thing CDOs meant. The traders are back at it again, which is why I'm warning you that the same thing is going to happen again. Whatever goes up must come down, and that includes the stock market, home values, and the price of crude oil and every other commodity people hold dear. How many little Madoffs are out there right now running scams on you? I'll answer my own question: all the millennials who graduated from college in the last decade think they're smarter than the manipulators and frauds who came before. They're not. They're educated but stupid. And greedy. And entitled. So what makes you think it won't happen again?

I read an interesting article called "High Risk Investment That Brought Down the U.S. Economy Returns, with a New Name." It was written by the far-left news organization—or should I say propaganda machine—ThinkProgress, which is funded by that criminal anarchist George Soros. Normally you'd think I would dismiss something from that source, but in this particular case it's right. The article opens with a great paragraph that says, "When a restaurant fails a health code inspection, sometimes the easiest thing to do is close up shop, let people forget what happened, then slap a new sign on the door and reopen under a new name. That's essentially what the world's biggest banks are doing with a complex, high-risk investment product that helped destroy the global economy less than eight years ago. Goodbye, 'collateralized debt obligations [CDOs].' Hello, 'bespoke tranche opportunities [BTOs].'" Then the article talks about the banks that are now selling bespoke tranche opportunities. Sales of those leapt from $5 billion in 2013 to $20 billion in 2014.

Can you believe it? In 2010, the total on-paper value of derivative contracts worldwide was $1.4 *quadrillion*, or twenty-three times the total economic output of the entire planet. Talk about fiscal conservatism. I'm a fiscal conservative, but I have to agree with the far Left when it criticizes this. It's that simple. For conservatives to dismiss everything that the Left says is as foolish as their dismissing everything I say. They're idiots if they do that. To say that *everything* the far Left says is garbage is wrong (although, generally, it *is* garbage, class warfare, race warfare, economic warfare, etc.). Sometimes it says something right, and this is 100 percent right.

Bernie Madoff, the collapse of the housing bubble— it's fascinating to have seen it once, and it's fascinating that we are about to live through it again and no one's doing anything about it. Again. The same exact elements are in place for another collapse, and it's going to happen right after a Republican is elected. That is the game that's being played out. We've had eight years of a corrupt criminal Democrat called Barack Obama, and that collapse is the next play in the game plan. We're all fed up with him, we know what he is, and we're saying, "Yeah, we need a Republican." So we're going to get a Republican, and then the economy's going to blow up and people will blame it on the Republicans.

This is the way the game is played. Before Obama we had eight years of another lawless and soulless bumbler, Bush, and in the last four months of his regime I said watch out for what's coming. I said Bush is a fiscal socialist, and you haven't seen what he's going to do yet. What happened was somewhat predictable. Then we got Obama and two terms of his anticapitalist, anti-American organization. He'll leave scot free; nothing will happen under his watch, other than the start of World War III against Islamofascism. A slow burner, that one. We'll have a combination of an economic collapse and World War III if the wrong candidate, one who attacks Russia, is elected. If the right Republican is elected, we might avoid both.

In some ways, *The Big Short* falls a little short. It tells how all those crooks brought down the housing market and who made money on it. But it doesn't name all the people involved who made billions. I was waiting for something, even a credit roll of the real robber barons. The movie didn't do that, it didn't even name the head of the SEC, who should be in prison, in my opinion.

Why am I angry at that oversight? Why did the movie and the interview with Madoff make me so angry? Because I believe an economic collapse is going to happen again. Some people don't know what happened, but it did happen. What actually happened? How did people with no credit, no credit history, even get a mortgage? Why was the bank giving you a mortgage if you couldn't pay for it? When I was a youngster and I bought my first house, I had to save for years to earn the down payment and then to pay the mortgage off. I used $9,000, my life savings, to make a down payment on a house in the Bay Area that cost $45,000. It was everything I had. That little house I bought in Fairfax, California, was the biggest thing in my life. I knew I was getting a toehold in America. I had one child at the time. I knew I had to buy something, and to get a mortgage I had to put down 20 percent of the value of the house. Not 18 percent, not 19.5 percent: if you didn't put down 20 percent, you weren't getting a mortgage from a bank. They were very tightly run.

Today, forget about it. But back then, just before the housing bubble burst, banks were giving mortgages to people who certainly not only couldn't qualify, and not just mortgages: they also handed out building loans that invited buyers to cheat. I knew a guy who bought a house in southern California for $1.25 million. While paying off the mortgage, he obtained a builder's loan for another million bucks that allowed him to renovate the place—but he didn't have to pay off *that* loan until he finished construction. Which meant he could hold off putting in the last nail, the last floor tile, until the place was sold. What happened? He held off on that last bit of renovation and put the place on the market for $2.6 million. It didn't sell. It continued not to sell. He defaulted on the mortgage. The bank repossessed. The house eventually sold for $1 million. The bank lost twice: once on the mortgage and once on the entire building loan.

The banks went bust but not the bankers. The lenders didn't care if buyers didn't qualify, as long as they got their commissions. They were giving mortgages to strippers who had five, six houses. Everyone was a real estate developer. Everyone thought they were mini–Donald Trumps. I'm not putting Donald down, but people thought they were big-shot investors. In the 1970s and 1980s, everyone thought he was a financial genius. Everyone thought he was a financial wizard because house values were going up.

I'm lucky. I'm able to be interested in the Madoff scam story because I wasn't touched by it. I'm not an investor. I don't invest money in anything. I don't trust investments. I never have. I own gold. I don't trust people with my money. I'm the kind of guy who wishes that banks were paying interest again. I'd rather have all my money in a bank. I'd even take 3 percent interest. Give me a 2.5 percent return, even, not a minus one, which is where they're going because of the false economy we're in. Why do you think we have 0 percent interest? Why do you think that Janet Yellen, the Federal Reserve chair, is keeping interest rates so low? Why do you think the World Bank is in a conspiracy with Yellen? Why do you think the national banks are keeping interest rates at zero or less than zero? Because the whole thing is a Ponzi scheme about to collapse on us.

The minute the banks permit a dime of interest to be made, people will put their money into banks again and try to make a little on their capital. The Fed doesn't want that. It wants you to keep the money in the economy. It wants you to keep pumping money out by buying stuff you don't really need. That's one of the theories of the kind of economic system we're in now, and eventually it has to lead to a crash.

We keep hearing "Government's bad—government's bad. They lost, too bad, let them go into the gutter." There's something wrong with that mantra. When you have a government that moves in and helps people have a roof over their head, that's bad, too? That's not pure enough conservatism for you? You'd rather have people in the gutter living in a cardboard box? See, this is the problem of people living in theory rather than in reality. The reality is that home owners would rather stay in their houses with government help than live in a cardboard box.

According to my good friend Craig Smith, the loans that were made, which the lenders knew up front were bad, were referred to as "ninja loans"—no interest, no job, no assets. A buyer could put nothing down and never make a payment. The originators knew the loans would fail, so they packaged them and sold them as securities. It was a fraudulent fiduciary instrument, but we have them back again—back again with fraudulent fiduciary instruments under the great con man currently in the White House. Here we are. The same thing again.

I am guesstimating that it will happen right after a Republican takes the White House next January. It's the game that's played—it's a show game. Eight years of Dems, and they throw the White House to Republicans and then blow the economy. Or eight years of Republicans, and then look at what Bush did: blew the economy, took the cash out of the Ponzi scheme, and his friends got very, very rich. Much richer than they had been. What happened right after that? Bingo, we got Obama, who "rescued" us.

Now it's going to be the same thing in reverse. I expect that this economy will continue to chug along on false money until December or so, maybe into January. Then the plug will be pulled after the really powerful people have pulled their money out of the Ponzi scheme and those people will be protected from holding the bag.

I don't know how to insulate against it. I could say "Buy gold," and I wouldn't be lying to you. What else are you going to do to hedge your money? Buy a wheat farm in Saskatchewan? Maybe. That might not be a bad idea. The Chinese are doing it. The Chinese are buying up the Chicago Stock Exchange, they are buying our farmland in the Midwest.

What a great nation this is, isn't it? What sane nation on Earth sells its own breadbasket to a foreign nation that's not exactly friendly to us? Tell me what sane nation has no laws to stop this.

It's called wildcat capitalism. That's the technical term. I have another term for it, just a word, actually.

Stupidity.

A WELCOME REVOLUTION COMES TO AMERICA

Revolution comes to America.

That's one of the themes of this book, and it's a theme you won't find anywhere else. That's because most people are afraid to acknowledge it, afraid to go against the liberals in the mainstream media. The reason I say "Revolution comes to America" is that the soul of America is plainly up for grabs. As I've said many times, Donald Trump represents America's best hope, maybe our only hope. The Democratic Party represents the new world socialist revolution. If you disagree, study the history of communism and see how the first step is always to bring about socialism, which eventually will become communism.

In her speeches, Clinton and her surrogates, such as Elizabeth Warren and Nancy Pelosi, are acting as though there's a Republican right-wing government running America. The truth is, we've had a radical psychotic left-wing government for eight straight years. And if Clinton wins the election, even though Obama will retire from his current position, he will continue to wield power behind the scenes. Do you not think that he will be held in godlike esteem by his erstwhile voting block?

Shall I go down the list of what might happen after they seize your guns and they release the thugs from Black Lives Matter into the streets of America, having armed them as their private army? If you think that sounds crazy, tell me when I've been wrong before. Do you remember the police executed in Dallas, Georgia, and Tennessee by haters who are black?

The rich have never been richer than they are today. But how can that be, if Obama is a socialist? In order to understand the answer to that question, you have to know a little bit about history. There have been many examples of dictators who have made certain that the richest people in their nation became richer under them.

Consider Hitler's success. Hitler won only 33 percent of the vote when he took over the Reichstag, so how did he survive and gain traction in the early years, when he didn't have absolute power? He made certain that the industrialists of his time, such as the Krupps, the steel fortune magnates who manufactured weapons, would get giant government contracts to rebuild the German military.

Next, if you ask yourself how Google, Microsoft, Facebook, and other gigantic firms get away with triple-Dutch tax dodges that let them slash their overseas tax rates to the low single digits, you'll see that the answer is that Obama lets them get away with it. Obama is not a socialist at all when it comes to cronyism. That is the big lie. Obama, Google, Microsoft, and the others complain about inequality in order to distract the public while they rob you by committing tax dodges, just as any pickpocket would direct your attention away from the hand that steals your wallet.

If Hillary Clinton becomes president of the United States in 2017, we'll have more of the same.

Under President Hillary, you can expect continued crony capitalism for herself, socialism for the little people. You know she's going to be looking out for the banks. You know how many millions of dollars they paid her—not her campaign, *her*—for a few speeches.

The big banks are totally in bed with the Democrats. And this tumor is not just benign, it's cancerous. What big banks and big industry want in return for their money is protection—protection to keep money circulating in their own little system. Small businesses and innovation threaten the positions of the fat cats at the top—and I mean Google, Facebook, and all the other corporations we hail as innovative geniuses. They haven't been that for years. They've secured their position at the top, and they're buying protection for themselves against anyone else being able to climb that ladder. For the rest of us, it's Obama-style socialism.

Don't be fooled by the way Hillary cozies up to Elizabeth Warren. Do you really think Hillary gives a damn about someone who might damage her relationship with Wall Street? That said, there is one way Hillary Clinton would benefit by picking Sister Elizabeth as her running mate: to get Warren out of the Senate, where that self-proclaimed one-fifth Cherokee can push her fingers into every pie cooling on the ledge. Hillary would be smarter putting her somewhere where she could keep an eye on her, keep her out of mischief.

I hope the nation is smarter than giving her this office.

The revolution is here in America. The soul of America is up for grabs. I have a friend from England who just came over here, and he said, "You should see what's going on in England right now." He said that in London, people are walking with their heads down. The city's new Muslim mayor, Sadiq Khan, has conquered that nation like Saladin, the warlord who battled the Crusaders. Everyone's feeling defeated.

The same thing is happening in the United States. If you walk around today in New York, San Francisco, Dallas, Phoenix, Chicago, Miami, or whatever city you're in, will you see people walking with their heads held high? No, you won't. People are walking around keeping their heads as close as they can to their shoulders, and it's not just because they're texting. It's because they are afraid. They are fearful of what Obama has unleashed upon society. He has turned street thugs into victims and the police into a neutral force. That leaves the "victims" free to attack the rest of us. Stabbings are way up in New York as I write this. Coincidence?

This devil in the White House has neutralized the police and unleashed street thugs onto American society. This is just the beginning, and the people know it. This is step one of the revolution that has arrived in America.

I want to tell you something about communism. You can find it right in *The Communist Manifesto*, which was originally published in London at the beginning of the revolutions of 1848. *The Communist Manifesto* is a carefully articulated guide for the struggle that arises when capitalism and private industry create a dependent, subservient working class. But what does that actually mean? It means nothing. The authors, Karl Marx and Friedrich Engels, were two idiots. They were two spoiled-rotten rich kids who didn't like other rich people and came up with an idealistic view of the world in which the peasants who were working in the factories and on the farms would own the factories and the farms, and then everyone would have a wonderful life. In the same way, the trust funders in Pacific Heights think the world will be great after a communist revolution.

Has it ever worked out well when the peasants ran the factories? Consider the grocery co-ops in Berkeley, California; Cambridge, Massachusetts; and others that followed their model as a result of the post-1960s fervor for revolution. The lame-brained idiots at Harvard and Berkeley wanted communism—they wanted the workers like the supermarket clerks and the guys who stacked cans on the shelves to own the market. How did the co-ops work out? They didn't. They went out of business. And they went out of business because the workers couldn't manage the supermarkets. Moreover, thievery was at an all-time high, just as it is in salad bars today from all of the left wingers in this country who think it's their right to steal vegetables out of a salad bar because they perceive the company that owns the salad bar to be ripping them off. And not just ripping them off but also suppressing the illegal immigrants who pick the lettuce and gather the tomatoes that are being served. Right on, you jackasses.

The socialism/communism rhetoric of Bernie Sanders is still resonating with the morons among the young, the uneducated, and the "educated" (brainwashed), because revolution has come to America. It's coming from Sanders and Clinton. It's coming from the Catholic Church.

But it's not coming from me. We are going to stop this revolution and replace it with one of our own. Just like Obamacare: repeal and replace. We are going to save America together. We are not going to sit here whining and wringing our hands. If the time comes, we will be in the streets, because we are going to stop them. I will not die on this earth and leave this country in ruins for my granddaughter to inherit because we were too cowardly to stand up for what we believe. You may think that you can just listen to the radio or read the newspapers or read blogs and stop this happening. You are wrong. You are going to have to put yourself out there. You are going to have to do what they're starting to do in Europe—stand up to the communists—or we're not going to have a nation.

If you think you're immune because you're not a rich person, you're crazy. Let me paraphrase the old saying for you.

First, they will come for the rich, but you are not rich, and so you will not stand up for the rich. Then they will come for the middle class, but you are not even middle class, so you won't stand up for the middle class. Then, when they start to come for the poor, there will be no one left to stand up for you, because everyone else will have been taken out already. That is how the system works. The communists eat their own. They start to kill one another. They take everything from everyone, and they produce nothing. That's Bernie Sanders and the American socialism movement in a nutshell. Do you know how many people died under communism in the last century in the Soviet Union, in China, in Cuba, in Asia? Do you know how many people died in the slave-labor camps, having been sent to the gulag for being politically incorrect?

Do you even know what the phrase "politically incorrect" actually means? We know that "politically correct" means handling words and sentences as though they were eggshells. By extension, politically incorrect simply means you're prepared to make an omelet. But you don't know who the monsters are, the ones behind the curtain who are trying to control your thoughts, your words, and your actions. You don't know what they want to do when they have total and absolute power. Many of you are Americans who have grown up in a spoiled nation—a nation without any problems and without any history. There is a new generation of brainwashed individuals who don't know anything about anything, and many of you are part of it. But I am from a different time, a different generation. I am from an America that had problems, an America that knew its history, an America that understood its present.

You bought this book because my mind has not been altered by the brainwashing of America, and that is one reason I am able to provide clear insights. The brainwashed generation is largely unaware that the soul of America itself is up for grabs. But it's as clear as crystal to me. The Democratic Party represents a new socialist-Islamist revolution. But the people of the brainwashed generation think it represents them. It doesn't. It represents a means of controlling them.

In the original *Communist Manifesto*, Marx and Engels described their theories of how the capitalist society of their time would be replaced first by socialism and then by communism. The youth of America who cheered for the grumpy old devil "Bernie" know nothing about history, and therefore they are condemned to repeat it. My friends, you who say it can't happen here: it is already happening here. You think you have a media that would never permit that to happen? It happened in Oregon. Oregon state police troopers, backed up by the thugs from the federal government, killed a man who was protesting on federal land. And very few in the media covered it. So try again to say it can't happen here. It can happen here. It is happening here.

In a quiet way, little by little, a communist revolution is happening right here in our country. Police are being knocked over like bowling pins across the nation by you-know-who and his acolyte, Loretta Lynch. Before her it was the worst attorney general in American history, Eric Holder. A gunman at a Panera Bread restaurant in Maryland shot and killed two deputies in February 2016. You cannot find a description or photo of the gunman. The piece of garbage opened fire on law enforcement officers, but the media did not show him to us.

Why are they withholding information like this? Because they've been empowered or commissioned to do so. How much lower does it get than a street thug like Al Sharpton having been into and out of the White House thirty-five, forty times, visiting this corrupt communist president of ours?

The smiling man in the White House and Al Sharpton— the "activist" who, without a scintilla of evidence, became a celebrity when he loudly backed a black girl, Tawana Brawley, who falsely accused six white men of rape? If someone had told me in the 1970s that this slithering white-hating con man would have a television show, that he would be into and out of the White House dozens of times, that he would pick the attorney general, that he would be sitting down with Bernie Sanders, the agitator from the New York gutters, at a restaurant in Harlem, I would have said, "You're crazy. It's impossible that anyone would take this gutter snipe seriously."

It just shows what has happened to America. It shows that the world is upside down. The best people are rejected and called right-wing maniacs, and the left-wing vermin are now running the country, from the media to the White House.

I'm still talking about it on the radio. I'm still writing these books. But that could change. Nothing is forever. If you think these voices of freedom are permanently here for you, you're mistaken. There are strong forces at work right now trying to get people like me silenced. In ways you would not imagine, they are trying to silence the voices that are speaking loudly against this one-world government revolution. One day you may find when you wake up that those forces have won and succeeded for reasons, and in ways, you won't want to believe.

Revolution has come to America. But why would a billionaire like the comedian and actor Larry David put himself out there for a socialist/communist like Bernie Sanders? Shouldn't he understand that if a commie wins, income taxes are going to be up to around 95 percent? Does Larry David want to pay 95 percent of his income to the federal government? I don't think so, but he may know something that we don't know. He may know what Microsoft knows. He may know what Facebook knows. He may know what many very wealthy people in this country know, such as Warren Buffett, which is that they don't pay the same taxes as the workingman.

Most of us pay more than our full and fair share of our income to the federal government. Here in the communist state of California under the great moonbeam of a governor Jerry Brown, high earners pay 15 percent of their income to the state, on top of 39 percent or 40 percent in federal taxes. So if we round it off, 40 percent and 15 percent is 55 percent of their income right off the top that goes to the gangsters who run the federal and state governments.

The United States has the highest corporate income tax in the entire world. There is no other nation on Earth that penalizes corporations as much as this country does. Then you get guys who take their businesses overseas and pay very little in American taxes. Or they derive their income from private corporations that pay them very little taxable income and pick up most of their living costs as deductible expenses! They are all for socialism. They love socialism because it doesn't cause them any problems. It causes problems only for other people. It actually helps them by placating the people on the bottom and keeping those at the bottom from eating the ones at the top alive. And it brings them cheap labor, such as IT workers from India. In other words, if you buy off the poor with handouts in a welfare state, what you're doing, in plain English, is buying protection against them breaking into your house and killing you. The rich who hide their corporate profits overseas are in favor of a welfare state because they feel the welfare state keeps the dangerous lower classes away from them, at least until the middle class runs out of money.

There is a very complicated reason for all of this, but the fact of the matter is that we are facing a real danger here and now. What is the difference between the middle class in America now and the people in Russia who were very poor and starving when Marx and Engels put out *The Communist Manifesto*? Actually, there are a couple of differences. One: There is no starvation in America—people here have never been so fat. They're fat and lazy and complacent. Two: We have guns. The paupers in Russia were not allowed to have guns. That is why the socialists have a gleam in the eye when they talk about taking away your weapons. The only thing that stands between them and absolute power is achieving a disarmed America, the kind of America that Thomas Jefferson warned us against. That is why the Second Amendment is the foundation of all the other amendments, and that is why the Second Amendment is being attacked. That is why the Left has a vendetta against the private ownership of weapons.

But the Left can't disarm America—only America can disarm America. So little by little, through propaganda in the media, through brainwashing and manipulation, Americans are loosening their grip on the Second Amendment. Americans are speaking out against the cornerstone of their own Constitution.

Fidel Castro took over Cuba because the people had no weapons under President Batista. Fulgencio Batista was so corrupt, so ruthless, that he couldn't afford to allow his people to be armed. But Castro had guns, and he used them. The Muslims who slaughtered so many innocents in Paris could do so because nobody in the *Charlie Hebdo* building, no one in the dance hall, had a weapon, and even the Paris police are unarmed. In Nice, the terrorist was finally prevented from committing further mayhem by *armed* police. There is only a certain division of the police in Paris that is allowed to have weapons. Into that breach entered the Muslims, who somehow found a way to get weapons.

Guns stop tyrants, too. That's why the one thing that the Left has been focused on is taking your weapons, and this is for obvious reasons.

When I was much younger I was cheated because I was told that if I studied and if I was good, I would have jobs and wages. When I grew up, my future was put on hold by the Left, not by the Right. My future was put on hold not by the capitalists but by the socialists in the ACLU and the universities. That's the paradox that the young don't understand. They're being promised a bill of goods that can never be delivered.

Yet there is hope. I call them the Eddies.

THE SLEEPING GIANT WILL AWAKEN: HOW EDDIE WILL SAVE AMERICA

On a Tuesday morning in late March of this year, I woke up, turned the TV on, and saw sickening scenes from the Brussels airport, scenes of blood, faces blown off, and babies crying. Then I heard the statement from the Islamofascists saying that "all the people of Belgium are soldiers, which is why we attacked them; there are no innocent civilians because they are all soldiers, because they are bombing our brethren in our homeland."

I won't ask how a baby can be a soldier, because the mind of an Islamofascist is not rational.

If this rant sounds familiar, it is because it's the kind of justification the Nazis used in their blitzkrieg invasion of Poland and the total conquest of Europe. I first wrote the word "Islamofascist" many years ago. People have used other words, such as jihadis and radical Muslims, but they are Islamofascists, they are the new Nazis, the Nazis of our time. Instead of wearing a swastika, instead of marching to a German band, instead of reading *Mein Kampf*, they are using different music and a different book. I'll leave it in those general terms. To discuss them further invites the kind of analysis that those subhumans don't deserve.

After I woke up and saw those images, I had a very difficult morning of reflection. Ultimately I said to myself, "You know, I've got to do my job today."

I've had other days like that since then. The terrorist from Tunisia who slaughtered scores of innocents in Nice, France, on Bastille Day 2016. Those two horrible days in June—two different events, one a nightclub shooting in Orlando, Florida, and another a bombing of an airport in Turkey. Then the assassination of police in Dallas and other cities in July by black racists. The attacks are coming faster and faster, and the scenes of carnage on TV are getting worse. And each time I wake up and think, "I've got to do my job today." I also think, "I wish to dear God that Obama would do his!"

But I'm only one man. And I'm not bulletproof.

Let's start with that. I'm just a man with a microphone, but I know history, and I also know what is going to be done. I can guarantee you as I am sitting here writing this that change is occurring, a shift from complacency. The change has been occurring since Donald Trump appeared on the scene. There is a sleeping giant that is awakening, and the sleeping giant who is going to effect this change is the blue-collar white man. The Japanese realized that after they bombed Pearl Harbor. One of the admirals said—and I'm paraphrasing here—that all they'd succeeded in doing was to wake a sleeping giant and fill it with terrible resolve.

I used to call those citizens, these proud Americans, the Eddies of the world. It's just a name, a common Christian name, but it embodies that which is the best in us. The Eddies who fought in World War II. The Eddies who put down their saws and ceased to be carpenters or electricians or farmers and went and fought the Nazi *Übermenschen*, the Supermen, as they called themselves. And every man who defeated that Superman will never forget it. *Everyman* defeated *Superman*.

Then when Eddie came home from winning World War II, he built the United States into the greatest country on Earth in the 1950s. The greatest nation in the history of the world.

Then along came the human plagues, the vermin I talked about earlier—the shyster William Kunstler, the degenerate Alan Ginsberg, the drug pusher Timothy Leary, and Bella Abzug, who had her own special brand of feminist supremacy. There were the militant Black Panthers, whom even Martin Luther King, Jr., couldn't stand. And this group of evildoers, these left-wing drug peddlers and social peddlers, destroyed the will of America. They twisted the entire American mind.

Some people think the twisting started with the beatniks. Go, man, go, huh? With the bongo drums and the beards and the sandals? It didn't. They were basically harmless, reading poetry in coffeehouses and on street corners. Even as a kid, I didn't pay much attention to them. But they were right about one thing: it went, man, went. Those days are over. Good-bye, beatniks and socialists and degenerates. Now we have to pick up the pieces because Eddie is still here.

Eddie had children, never forget it. And not all of Eddie's boys became girls. Not all of Eddie's boys went to Harvard. Not all of Eddie's boys went to NYU. Not all of Eddie's girls went to Columbia Law School. Eddie's boys and girls are still in America, and they still have American values.

Those people, those blue-collar families, are still the majority, they're still the backbone of this country. They didn't vote in the last presidential election because Barry Obama and Mittens Romney didn't speak to them. But I can guarantee you as I sit here that they're going to vote in the next one. And when that sleeping giant, those former nonparticipants in the political process, finally elect their leader, you're going to see a change unlike any you've seen in your lifetime. Whether you like it or not.

They'll vote because they'll finally realize that the West is being savaged from within by militant Islamists and secularists from the left. They'll vote because if they do not, Christian beliefs will be stamped out and the West will be stamped out along with them. They'll vote because they'll finally understand what John Adams, America's second president, was talking about when he said, "Our Constitution was made only for a moral and religious people. It is wholly inadequate to the government of any other."

You are hearing loud outcries against Donald Trump and the rising, forceful Eddies. You're hearing them described as bigots, racists, antiwomen, anti-Semites, and homophobic. But those voices will eventually dim. The shouters will be reduced to the marginal characters that they've always been. They'll be put back into the boxes they came from.

How do I know this? Because the Eddies will come to our defense one more time. They will stand shoulder-to-shoulder to honor the legacy of those who built this nation, who fought its wars, who bowed in prayer in a rich variety of faiths, and who raised the families that are the backbone of America.

And when they do, I can guarantee you that this nation—that this world—will be a safer place . . . even for the lunatic fringe.

NOTES

67, 69–71, 73: Alexey Eremenko, "Back in the U.S.S.R.? How Today's Russia Is like the Soviet Era," NBC News, Nov. 30, 2015, http://www.nbcnews.com/news/world/back-u-s-s-r-how-todays-russia-soviet-era-n453536.

113: Ingrid Carlqvist, "Sweden Close to Collapse," Gatestone Institute, Oct. 17, 2015, http://www.gatestoneinstitute.org/6697/sweden-collapse.

125: Deena Yellin, "Defiance: The Bielski Brothers Heroic Tale of Survival," Chabad.org, http://www.chabad.org/library/article_cdo/aid/853108/jewish/Defiance.htm.

139–40: Craig Bannister, "VIDEO: WH Censors French President Saying 'ISLAMIST Terrorism,'" MRCTV, April 1, 2016, http://www.mrctv.org/blog/video-wh-censors-reference-islamist-terrorism-french-president.

211: Simon Kent, "Le Pen: Europe's Migrant Flood Equals 'Barbarian Invasions of 4th Century,'" Breitbart, Oct. 6, 2015, http://www.breitbart.com/london/2015/10/06/ le-pen-europes-migrant-flood-equals-barbarian-invasions-4th-century/.

218: Neville Chamberlain, "Peace for Our Time," Sept. 30, 1938, Britannia Historical Documents, http://www. britannia.com/history/docs/peacetime.html.

273: Alan Pyke, "High Risk Investment That Brought Down the U.S. Economy Returns, with a New Name," Think Progress, Feb. 5, 2015, http://thinkprogress. org/economy/2015/02/05/3619325/bespoke-tranche-opportunities-are-your-god-now-america/.